T0196651

COUNSELS FROM MY HEART

༄༅། །སྐུབས་རྗེ་རོ་རྗེ་འཆང་བདུད་འཇོམས་རིན་པོ་ཆེ་
འཇིགས་བྲལ་ཡེ་ཤེས་རོ་རྗེའི་ཞལ་གདམས་
ཕྱོགས་བསྡུས་ཡེ་ཤེས་རབ་འབར་
བཞུགས།།

པཎྜི་ཀུ་རའི་སྐྲ་བསྒྱུར་མཐུན་ཚོགས་ནས་
སྐྲ་བསྒྱུར་ཞུས།།

Dudjom Rinpoche

COUNSELS
FROM MY
HEART

*Translated by the Padmakara
Translation Group*

SHAMBHALA
Boston & London
2003

Shambhala Publications, Inc.
Horticultural Hall
300 Massachusetts Avenue
Boston, Massachusetts 02115
www.shambhala.com

© 2001 by the Padmakara Translation Group

All rights reserved. No part of this book may be
reproduced in any form or by any means, electronic
or mechanical, including photocopying, recording,
or by any information storage and retrieval system,
without permission in writing from the publisher.

Printed in the United States of America

⊗ This edition is printed on acid-free paper that meets the
American National Standards Institute z39.48 Standard.
♻ Shambhala Publications makes every effort to print on recycled
paper. For more information please visit www.shambhala.com.
Distributed in the United States by Penguin Random House LLC
and in Canada by Random House of Canada Ltd

The Library of Congress catalogues the hardcover edition
of this book as follows:
Bdud-'joms 'Jigs-bral-ye-shes-rdo-rje, 1904–
    Counsels from my heart / Dudjom Rinpoche.—1st ed.
        p.   cm.
    Includes bibliographical references.
    ISBN 978-1-57062-844-3 (cloth)
    ISBN 978-1-57062-922-8 (pbk.)
    1. Spiritual life—Rñin-ma-pa (Sect)   2. Rñin-ma-pa
(Sect)—Doctrines   I. Title.
BQ7662.6 B386   2001
294.3′420423—dc21   2001020829

To Kyabje Dudjom Rinpoche's consort,
Sangyum Rigdzin Wangmo,
with prayers for her long life and the fulfillment of all
  her wishes,
this translation is gratefully and respectfully dedicated.

Contents

P R E F A C E

Om svasti
The second Buddha, Padmakara,
In this darkened age
Appeared again in human guise
As Dudjom Rinpoche, my lord,
Drodul Lingpa Yeshe Dorje.
His name so sweet to hear sends forth
A ray of splendor in the world;
To him my heart bows down!
His deep instructions have distilled
Undying nectar from myriad teachings,
Marvelous excellence and sacred witness
Of the Buddha's Dharma!
To hear them frees the mind,
To think of them transports
My heart with joy!

These are my verses of welcome for some of the oral teachings of the lord of mandalas, Kyabje Dudjom Dorje Chang, Drodul Lingpa Jigdrel Yeshe Dorje—instructions that have fallen like a gentle rain upon the aspirations and abilities of those who might be trained. And here they have been gathered in a little book.

I have no doubt that this quintessence of the profound teachings, faithfully translated in France by the Padmakara Translation Group, is able to cure the sickness of the afflictions for all of us, Buddhist or not, who have been born in this age of degenerate ideas and violent negative emotion. I am sure that these teachings will inspire the minds of everyone, bringing them happiness. I pray that you will read and think about them often.

Ignorant Wakindra Dharmamati, monk of Shakyamuni, who goes by the name of Zarong Trulshik Shatrul, wrote this in Trashi Pelbar Ling, La Sonnerie, Dordogne, France on the auspicious twenty-fifth day of the eleventh lunar month, 1999.

Jayantu!

*T*RANSLATORS' NOTE

The main part of this book consists of a series of discourses given by Kyabje Dudjom Rinpoche.[1] One of them dates from as early as 1962, but on the whole, they were delivered during the 1970s, some in the East and some in the West. The talks were recorded, and were later transcribed and published in a small volume, probably in Kathmandu. A copy of this book was given to Padmakara with a request from Dudjom Rinpoche's consort, Sangyum Rigdzin Wangmo, for it to be translated. Thus it is thanks to her, and with her gracious permission, that these wonderful teachings are being made available to Western readers.

Unlike the other three schools of Tibetan Buddhism, which sprang up in the period following the persecution of King Langdarma and which are organized, in the main, around a particular leader or hierarch, the Nyingmapas, whose tradition goes back to the foundation of Buddhism in Tibet, did not form a single monolithic body. Elaborate institutions and complicated administration are somewhat foreign to the Nyingma spirit. The tradition evolved in a loose, uncentralized manner, producing a wide spectrum of teaching and practice, principally associated, as Dudjom Rinpoche says, with six great monasteries and their innumerable branch monasteries. This at least was the situation before the Chinese invasion. But then disaster struck; the monasteries were destroyed and those who were able escaped to India. As a means of preserving the integrity of the tradition, it was thought necessary to nominate a single leader around whom the scattered remnants could rally. This was a new departure for the Nyingmapas, and yet it posed no problem. As a master of immense learning and realization, as a *tertön,* as an unquestioned authority on the Nyingma teachings and especially the Great Perfection, and as the acknowledged representative of Guru Padmasambhava himself, Dudjom Rinpoche was the unanimous choice. He was the object of spontaneous and universal veneration, and was duly recognized by the Dalai Lama as the leader of the Nyingmapas.

It was only indirectly, of course, that we Westerners, beginners in the practice, could vaguely glimpse the extent of his spiritual authority and his accomplishment as a master of the Great Perfection—the revered guru of many disciples who were themselves accomplished masters. But despite the humility and relaxed lightheartedness of Rinpoche's bearing, no one, when with him, could be unaware of being in the presence of a very great master, an embodiment of the teachings. As we often heard from the mouths of lamas and khenpos alike, "He simply *was* Guru Rinpoche."

All the more amazing then, that in addition to laboring tirelessly for the preservation and practice of the teachings among Tibetans in India, Nepal, and Bhutan, Dudjom Rinpoche took such a lively and compassionate interest in "foreign" disciples, both Eastern and Western. As the years passed, he traveled not only to the countries of South Asia and the Far East, but also to Europe and America. Like Guru Padmasambhava in Tibet, he established the Dharma in "distant barbarous regions," and according to the exacting standards of an authentic tradition. Finally, it was in Dordogne, France, that he chose to reside on a permanent basis. There, in January 1987, he passed away amid many marvelous signs, letting fall a stream of blessings that is still palpable.

For us Westerners, he was indeed a loving father. And although, as occasion required, he did not mince his words, and could speak sternly and to the point in appropriately colorful and graphic language, he was the personification of gentle kindness. His presence was a source of endless inspiration; his writings, the pattern of clarity and elegance. His oral teachings, as we hope this book will show, had the simple, uncluttered directness of true mastery, so accessible and clear. He was nevertheless, and as his brief autobiography indicates, a person of great modesty. Matter-of-fact about his training and work, he concealed his personal attainments beneath a veil of playful humor.

Dudjom Rinpoche holds a very special place for the members of the Padmakara Translation Group. Not only did he found his own teaching center at Laugeral, Dordogne, in 1980, but in the same year he gave his blessing to the first three-year retreat at Chanteloube, which he personally inaugurated and guided, giving many empowerments and essential teachings.

Working on this translation has been a great privilege and it is offered as a humble gesture of deep gratitude, however clumsy and imperfect. To the oral teachings contained in the original collection of transcripts, we have added a number of items that will perhaps be of interest to Western readers. These are a short autobiography, two poems, and a brief introduction to the Great Perfection. We are especially pleased to include this last item, which was translated in consultation with Kyabje Trulshik Rinpoche. It is included with his gracious permission.

Written in Dordogne, on the anniversary of Guru Rinpoche's birth,
August 2000

A CKNOWLEDGMENTS

The translators would like to thank, first of all, the anonymous transcriber and the publisher of the recordings of Dudjom Rinpoche's teachings. In addition, we owe a special debt of gratitude to Trulshik Rinpoche, who graciously composed the preface to the book and gave his blessing to the entire project. We are also very grateful to our teachers Pema Wangyal Rinpoche, Jigme Khyentse Rinpoche, and especially Rangdrol Rinpoche, who on numerous occasions gave us much help with the text and generally made the translation possible. Last but not least, we would like to thank our readers, Jenny Kane, Steve Gethin, and Vivian Kurz, for their generous help and valuable suggestions. The translation was made by Helena Blankleder and Wulstan Fletcher of the Padmakara Translation Group.

The Padmakara Translation Group gratefully acknowledges the generous support of the Tsadra Foundation in sponsoring the translation of this book.

COUNSELS FROM MY HEART

THE BUDDHADHARMA 1

A Talk Given by Kyabje Dudjom Rinpoche
to His Western Disciples

Faithful Dharma friends gathered here, I am very happy to be able to talk to you a little about the Buddha's teaching!

All of us here, human beings of this world, from every race and background, feel an instinctive and genuine devotion for the supreme Dharma. We have gained a clear confidence in it and have entered the door of the profound teachings. We are so very fortunate!

What we call the sacred Dharma is something unbelievably precious and difficult to find. Our present wish to commit ourselves to it, and the fact that we have all the favorable circumstances and good fortune of actually being able to practice—all this is happening to us thanks to the enormous reserves of merit we have generated in the past.

The Three Vehicles

What is the origin of this supreme teaching? It has come to us from the perfect Buddha, the fourth of the one thousand and two buddhas due to appear in the course of the Fortunate *kalpa*. And we ourselves are living at a time when his teaching still exists. Moreover, although all the buddhas are alike in expounding the Dharma of the three vehicles,[2] it was only Buddha Shakyamuni who revealed–in a period when the life span of humankind was about one hundred years–the diamond vehicle of Secret Mantra.

According to the fundamental doctrines of the *shravakas* and *pratyekabuddhas*, our teacher Shakyamuni was a person of sharp, superior faculties, who first accumulated merit for three immeasurable kalpas, purified defilements for a further three, and at length attained the perfection of buddhahood. According to this point of view, he was an ordinary man who achieved enlightenment through the accumulation of merit and the purification of defilements. The view of the Secret Mantrayana of the Great Vehicle, however, is that the Buddha actualized the *dharmakaya*, thus accomplishing his own fulfillment, innumerable kalpas in the past. It was his *rupakaya*, his body of manifestation, that compassionately descended into this world for the sake of others, appearing as Buddha Shakyamuni. An emanation of compassion, "coming from above,"[3] necessarily appears for the benefit of the inhabitants of this samsaric world, and, in order to help them, manifests in a form that harmonizes with their condition. This is why the Buddha displayed the twelve deeds of an enlightened being–descending from the heaven of Tushita, taking birth in this human world, and finally manifesting his enlightenment.[4]

Afterward, the Buddha turned the wheel of Dharma for the sake of beings, teaching according to their varying needs and particular outlook. For those with limited capacity of mind and a smaller stock of karmic fortune, he set forth the path of the shravakas and pratyekabuddhas, where the main emphasis is on the avoidance of nonvirtue in word and deed. For those with greater capacity and excellent merit, he gave the teachings of the Mahayana, where the emphasis is on mind-training, which is the cultivation of *bodhichitta*. Here the vows and precepts relating to body and speech are taught as auxiliaries. Finally, for those whose mental horizons and reserves of merit are even greater, and who are ready to receive them, the Buddha set forth the teachings of the resultant vehicle of the Secret Mantra of the Mahayana, which go far beyond the doctrines of the causal vehicles.[5]

Refuge and Bodhichitta

So, to begin with, what is it that brings us into the Buddha's teaching? What is the door through which we must enter, the "mental soil," so to speak, in which we can plant the seed of Dharma? It is taking refuge. This marks the difference between a Buddhist and a non-Buddhist, between one who is inside the teachings and one who is outside. To take refuge is to recognize the Three Jewels of Buddha, Dharma, and Sangha as one's unchanging protectors, and to turn to them sincerely and with full confidence. This opens the door of the Dharma at the very outset.

When we have taken refuge in the Three Jewels, what should our fundamental attitude be? We should understand that the whole of space is pervaded by living beings; there is not one of them that has not been, at one time or another, our father or our mother. We should recognize that they have been our parents and feel gratitude toward them for the love and kindness they have shown us. We should also realize that all these beings, once our mothers, are sinking in the ocean of the sufferings of samsara. We should cultivate the attitude of bodhichitta, taking the decision to practice the supreme Dharma for their sake. Bodhichitta is thus the fundamental preparation and basis of our practice of the path.

Those who have the attitude of shravakas or pratyekabuddhas are not able to appreciate that the whole of space is filled with beings who were once their parents, and that it is for their sake that they should practice Dharma. They are satisfied simply with the idea of freeing themselves from the ocean of samsaric sorrow. And it is in accordance with this ideal of individual liberation that they observe ethical discipline, abstaining from evil actions of word and deed. They spend their lives in the practice of purification and meditation, through which they reach the level of pratyekabuddha. This happens, however, only after practicing for as long as one measureless kalpa, or at least for three lives, sixteen lives, and so on.

People who have the attitude of the Mahayana think that it is somehow shameful to want liberation only for themselves, when other beings who were once their loving parents are sunk in the ocean of suffering. They are unable to imagine anything worse, and resolve to practice the Dharma in order to be able to lead beings, their parents, to liberation. They are determined to do this regardless of the consequences, and are ready to remain in samsara for as long as it takes to accomplish the task. This is the vast, great-hearted attitude that we too must have.

Nothing we do—not a single prostration or recitation of a single *mani*, not a single meditation on the stages of creation and perfection, no practice, no *sadhana*—should be without prayers of refuge and bodhichitta at the beginning, and prayers of dedication and aspiration at the end.

The sacred Dharma, as we have been saying, is ex-

tremely vast and profound, containing innumerable instructions. It is said that to suit the different mental
capacities of individuals, the Buddha set forth no less than
eighty-four thousand sections of doctrine. When we practice, our task is to condense all these teachings into a single,
essential point. But how are we to do this? In fact, although
the Buddha gave innumerable teachings, the crucial mes-
sage of all of them is contained in one verse:

> Abandon every evil deed,
> Practice virtue well,
> Perfectly subdue your mind:
> This is Buddha's teaching.

The Buddha did indeed say that we should not do evil
but practice virtue. Well, then, what *is* an evil action? An
act of body, speech, or mind is evil when it brings harm to
others. And as the Buddha said, we *must* refrain from doing
anything that injures others. Conversely, actions are positive or virtuous when they bring benefit to others.

What is the root of all this, the source of both good and
evil? The doer of all virtue is the mind, when it makes
positive use of body and speech, its servants. The doer of
all evil is also the mind, when it uses body and speech
negatively. The root and cause of good and evil is in the
mind itself. Nevertheless, in a sense, this mind of ours is

something unknown to us. It does anything and everything, like a lunatic running here and there at the slightest
impulse. This is how it accumulates karma.

The mind is the root of every defilement. It is *here* that
anger is born; and from anger, every kind of hurt and
injury to others: fighting, beating, and the rest. The mind
is the soil in which all this grows: all malevolence, envy,
desire, stupidity, arrogance, and so forth. That is why the
Buddha told us to get a grip on our minds. Having realized
that the mind is the root of all affliction, we must be vigi-
lant in keeping it under control, holding down our defilements as much as we can. We have to be completely
focused on this, gaining mastery of whatever arises.

The mind can move in a positive direction as well. It
can recognize the qualities of the Lama and the Three
Jewels, thanks to which it experiences faith, and so takes
refuge. Through the practice of the Dharma, the mind can
also accumulate the causes for its own liberation and that
of others. Therefore, since the mind is the root of both
good and evil, it stands to reason that it must be corrected
and transformed. The examination of one's mind is thus
the principal feature of the practice; the mind is the common concern of all the vehicles of Dharma. This is particularly true of the tantra teachings. Once again, it is the
mind that enters the mandala of the Secret Mantra of the
Vajrayana and accomplishes all the practices.

The Secret Mantra of the Vajrayana

It is thanks to the Lama, our spiritual friend, that we have been able to cross the threshold of the profound teachings of the sacred Dharma. We did not have the good fortune, defiled and impure as we were, to meet the Buddha in person while he was alive. But we have had the good fortune to encounter the Dharma, his teachings, and this is actually better than meeting him in person. These instructions, which reveal to us what we must do and what we must refrain from doing, have been given to us by our teacher. It is crucial to understand that we are incredibly fortunate to have been accepted by a spiritual friend. It is the Lama who opens our eyes to what we must do and what we must avoid. It is he who points out the defilements we must abandon, and in so doing, he fulfills the activity of the Buddha himself. If we truly assimilate and carry out all that he says with regard to actions to be done and actions to be avoided, we will attain our objective, namely liberation.

It is important to understand how to practice the Buddhadharma properly. We have to do it well, condensing all the hundreds of methods into a single point. If we do this, our practice will become easy and very effective. What is more, the teachings of Secret Mantra, the Vajrayana, have not yet vanished from the world. They still exist. To have entered them and to abide in them is our supreme good fortune. We are amazingly lucky.

Why, you may ask, are the Mantra teachings to be kept secret? It is not because of their profundity, but rather to preserve them from people of limited and narrow attitudes. The path of Secret Mantra has unusual features such as ease, rapidity, great subtlety, and skillful techniques. In other words, it is endowed with many methods, it is without difficulty, it is for those with sharp mental faculties, and its practice is very subtle. Those who are naturally fitted to the Secret Mantra will by this means attain the fruit of buddhahood easily and quickly. Indeed, the very word *mantra* combines the notions of ease and swiftness.

The difference between the view and practice of Secret Mantra and that of the other paths is often illustrated by the image of a field in which a poisonous plant has sprouted. People of little courage, narrow minds, and limited resourcefulness think that if they eat the poisonous plant, they will certainly die. So they cut down the plant and throw it far away. And fearing that new shoots might grow from the plant's root, they dig it up. This is what people without much courage do.

The poison in this image represents ignorance. And since even the tiniest fragment of the poisonous root must be removed from the soil and thrown away, it is evident that such people must go to a lot of trouble to extract it.

This is comparable to the way in which the fruit of liberation is attained by practicing according to the view of the shravakas and the pratyekabuddhas.

Now suppose an ingenious, stout-hearted person comes along and asks the people what they are up to. They will say that if the poisonous plant is allowed to grow, it will be very dangerous. Not only must they cut it down, they must uproot it so that no trace of it is left in the soil. Now, what will be the approach of the clever person? He will agree that the plant must be properly disposed of, but he will know that it is not necessary to go to such lengths to make sure that the plant stops growing. He will point out that the plant can be killed easily by pouring boiling water over its roots. His approach is similar to the way defilements are dealt with according to the Bodhisattva-yana. To remove defilements, it is not necessary to go through the same difficulties as the shravakas at the level of adoption and abandonment of actions. Nevertheless, in the Bodhisattvayana, it is still necessary to use antidotes. Meditating on love, for example, is a remedy for anger. Antidotes are certainly adopted with the understanding that they are different and separate from the defilements they are intended to cure.

What if a doctor were to come along and ask the people what they were doing? On being told that they were getting rid of the dangerous plant, he would say, "Ah, but I'm a doctor. I know how to make medicine from this plant. I can use this plant to make an excellent remedy to the very poison that it contains. Indeed, I have been looking for it for a long time. Give it to me. I'll take care of it." This doctor is like a practitioner of Secret Mantra. He can concoct powerful medicines from the poison. Such a practitioner does not need to go through the trouble of avoiding defilements, considering them distinct from the remedy. Defilements themselves can be transformed into wisdom. This is the path of Secret Mantra.

Finally, imagine that a peacock comes upon the poisonous plant. Without a moment's hesitation, it will eat it with great relish and its plumage will become even more ravishing. For the peacock, which represents the practitioners of the Great Perfection of the Secret Mantra, poisonous plants are not something to be shunned at all. Practitioners of the Great Perfection are aware that there is no such thing as a real, solid defilement to be abandoned. Just as the peacock consumes the poison, with the result that its feathers become more and more beautiful, the practitioner of Secret Mantra does not reject defilements but brings to perfection the enlightened qualities of the *kayas* and wisdoms. This gives us an idea of the differences between the greater and lesser paths.

Only a peacock is able to nourish itself on poison. In the same way, the teachings of the Great Perfection of the Secret Mantra are found in no other spiritual tradition. On the other hand, different people belong by their character to different paths, and these may be greater or lesser. It is essential for them to train according to their capacity, otherwise they will be in great danger. In order to be able to practice the Great Perfection, it is essential to be completely convinced, to be absolutely certain, of the view. For this reason, I am going to say a few words about it: the view of the Great Perfection of the Secret Mantra of the Mahayana.

The Great Perfection

The manner in which we, devoted yogis and yoginis, should practice the teaching of the Great Perfection has been taught by Guru Rinpoche, the Precious Master. He said that while our view should be that of the Great Perfection, *our actions should not get lost in the view.* What did he mean? The view is normally understood as the certainty that all phenomena, both of samsara and of nirvana, are empty. This, however, is something that we practitioners are not yet able to realize directly, and until we do, the fact is that we experience benefit and harm, virtue and nonvirtue, and the so-called karmic process of cause and effect. All this exists for us. So if, while still in our present condition, we go around saying, "Everything is empty. It's all one. There's no such thing as virtue, no such thing as sin," and if we do anything and everything we like, this is called "losing one's actions in the view." If this happens to us, it will be as Guru Rinpoche himself said. We will fall into the evil view of demons.

The view, then, refers to great emptiness. If we have a correct understanding of the ultimate status of phenomena, and if we are able to maintain and assimilate this through meditation, we will find in due course that dualistic perception will fall apart all by itself. There will come a moment when there is no such thing as benefit or harm, no such thing as happiness or sadness. It is then and only then that we will really have mastered the view. Guru Rinpoche said, "My view is higher than the sky, but my attention to actions and their results is finer than flour." We may well have an intellectual understanding of the view, the ultimate state of emptiness, but with regard to the practice, it is important to preserve this ultimate state continually, until our dualistic perceptions completely collapse.

On the other hand, Guru Rinpoche also said that we should not "lose our view in our actions." What did he mean here? Simply understanding and saying that things are empty does not make them empty. Our bodies and minds, and all the things that stimulate our thoughts, will stay just as they were; they won't just vanish! As a result, we may lose confidence in the view and concentrate exclusively on physical and verbal activities, dismissing the view as unimportant. If this happens, a clear realization of the view will never come to us. The teachings say therefore that we should avoid one-sided attitudes regarding the view and action. Like eagles soaring in space, we should be clearly convinced of the view, but at the same time we should heed the karmic principle of cause and effect, as finely as if we were sifting flour.

As Buddhists, we rely on the teachings of the Buddha, and must therefore have heartfelt confidence in the supreme Dharma. Whoever we are, we need to have a good heart, sincere and without deceit. At all times and on all occasions, we must maintain an irreversible trust in the sacred Dharma, and our minds must be steady and constant. These three things are our firm foundation: steady faith, sincere devotion, and constancy. Furthermore, whatever the Dharma contains, it is all Buddha's teaching. We must therefore have pure perception and an appreciation of *all* Dharma traditions, those of others as much as our own. We must respect them all. Finally, we must nourish within ourselves a constant, uninterrupted affection for our Dharma brothers and sisters.

The Three Supreme Methods

Whatever practices we do, whether the common ones of taking refuge and making prostrations, the various trainings in bodhichitta, the methods for purifying the defilements of body and speech, or the uncommon practices of the Secret Mantra (the visualization and recitation of

Vajrasattva, guru yoga, or meditation on the *yidam* deity), all that we do—and this is very important—should be accompanied by the three "supreme methods."

The first of these methods is the attitude of bodhichitta. All beings possess the *tathagatagarbha*, the seed of buddhahood, but this is obscured and veiled. As a result, they wander in samsara. The first method is therefore to be determined to liberate them from this ocean of suffering. The second supreme method is to have a mind free from conceptualization, which means to practice without distraction. Even if we make only a single prostration, we should not just go through the motions mechanically, with our thoughts and words elsewhere. On the contrary, we should practice with a concentrated mind, and never be carried away by distraction. The third supreme method is to conclude with dedication. Whatever merit has been generated must be dedicated for the sake of beings, who are as many as the sky is vast. In fact, if we forget to round off our practice with the excellent attitude of bodhichitta, dedicating the merit to others, this merit could be destroyed in a moment of strong anger or defilement. For this reason, all positive actions should immediately be followed by an act of dedication for the welfare of all beings. The benefits of this supreme method are immense; dedication renders merit inexhaustible and causes it to increase constantly.

What is the sign that someone has received the teachings of the supreme Dharma and is practicing them? Whoever has heard and absorbed the teachings becomes serene and self-possessed. Ours is not a tradition that inculcates anger and encourages us to fight; it does not encourage us to get involved with our defiled emotions. On the contrary, the Buddha has taught us to get rid of our defilements as much as possible. The point is that, having received the Dharma teachings, we should find when we examine ourselves, that, even though we may not have been able to eradicate our defilements totally, our anger has at least diminished a little. We should find that, even if we do get angry, we are less involved and are able to keep ourselves in check. This is the sort of sign we should be looking for. The sign that we are assimilating the teachings is an increase in serenity and self-control. It is said that if practitioners do not examine themselves frequently, and if they fail to practice correctly, the Dharma itself will lead them to the lower realms. Some people claim to have received the teachings, but they don't practice them. On the other hand, it is obviously impossible to eradicate defiled emotion just by listening to the teachings. We have been in samsara from beginningless time and are immersed in the habits of defilement. These cannot be whisked away by the mere act of listening to something. So turn inward and examine your minds. You should at least have a glimmer of understanding!

In addition, we have all entered the Vajrayana. We

have received profound empowerments and instructions
of the Secret Mantra. This is said to be very beneficial but
it is also very dangerous. Even if we are unable to bring
our practice to accomplishment, if we keep our *samaya*
unbroken, it is said that liberation will be achieved in
seven lifetimes. After crossing the threshold of the Secret
Mantra, however, if we ruin our samaya by displeasing the
Lama, causing havoc among our fellow Dharma practitioners and so on, the only possible destiny for us is the
vajra hell.[6] The saying goes that practitioners of Secret
Mantra either attain buddhahood or go to hell. There is
no third alternative. It's like a snake inside a cane: it must
go either up or down. There's no way out halfway! Think
carefully about the benefits and hazards of samaya, and
observe it purely and perfectly. To do this, it is crucial to
keep a close watch on your mind, a practice in which all
the essential points of the teachings are condensed. It is
vital to examine and watch your mind. You have all received instructions through the kindness of your teachers.
This is what your Dharma practice should be like.

Samsara and Ego-Clinging

But now I must tell you one or two things. In the mind of
everyone, of every living, sentient being, there is a fundamental nature or ground, the so-called *sugatagarbha*. This
is the seed of Samantabhadra, the seed of buddhahood.
Although this is something we all have, we do not recog-

nize it. It is unknown to us. This ground, which is our spontaneous awareness, has been with us "from the beginning." It is like a mirror. When someone with a happy face looks in a mirror, the reflection of a happy face appears. When someone with a sad face looks into it, a sad face appears. The primordial ground is just like a mirror.

The reflection of a person with a happy face looking into a perfectly clear mirror, the primordial ground, is like Samantabhadra, who awoke to his ultimate nature. Samantabhadra, it is said, "captured the citadel of the primordial ground, awoke, recognized his own nature, and was free." But we ordinary beings fail to recognize this nature, the mirrorlike primordial ground. For us, the situation is like someone with a downcast face looking into the mirror: a sad reflection appears! This is precisely what happens when, through our habit of samsara, the primordial ground is transformed into the so-called *alaya*. A subtle ego-apprehending consciousness emerges from it, and the sense of "I" and clinging to "I" manifest. When this happens, another mental state occurs, projected outward onto objects, which are perceived as being outside and separate from the mind.

The primary mechanism of "I-apprehension" may be compared to a house with six doors, corresponding to the six consciousnesses. This is how it works: "I-apprehension," the thought of "I," expands into other mental states.

Thus a second thought arises and is projected (let's say through one of the doors of the house) toward various patches of color that are the objects of the visual sense. After this, there is a thought of recognition: the object is identified and named as this or that. The apprehension of the characteristics of colors and so on, grasped as outer objects, is the definition of visual consciousness. Similarly, a consciousness projects onto objects of hearing, so that we hear sounds. Then other, even coarser, thoughts develop and run after the sound, recognizing it as this or that, this word, that word, apprehending it as pleasant or unpleasant. The coordinator of these thoughts is the auditive or ear consciousness. Then there is a consciousness that projects out, toward objects of smell. Steadily adverted to, these are apprehended as outer realities and are experienced as pleasant or unpleasant, and thus we have the smell consciousness. Again, another consciousness expands out toward objects of taste, apprehended as delicious or revolting, sweet or sour. This is the taste consciousness. Finally, there is a consciousness projected onto the body, the consciousness of touch, which apprehends physical contact, rough or smooth, as the case may be. We can see therefore that, based on the state of mind that thinks "I" is experienced as somehow inhabiting the body, which is in turn regarded as a single entity, the five kinds of consciousness project outward by means of the

five sense organs. There are six consciousnesses altogether: the five sense consciousnesses plus the mental consciousness, and it is thanks to these that samsara unfolds.

Samsaric activity proceeds apace and we remain in
delusion. The root of delusion is ignorance, and the root
of ignorance is ego-apprehension, the idea of "I." Samsara
occurs simply because we do not recognize our true nature. It is on account of this "I," this clinging to the notion
of self, that we conceive of "others." As a result, we enter
into subject-object relationships, and these prevent us
from escaping from samsara.

Because we have a sense of "I" and cling to self, pride
occurs. Because we cling to self, anger and the other emotional poisons arise. If we are practicing according to the
lower vehicles, we must discard these emotions by the
application of antidotes—remedies that vary according to
the poisons and sense objects in question. But for us practitioners of the Secret Mantra, only one supreme instruction is necessary, a single antidote that liberates
everything. We must acquire a deep conviction regarding
the true nature of phenomena. Once again, the root of
delusion is ignorance. And what is ignorance? It is clinging to self.

What Is the Mind?

Well, then, where is this self-clinging? That which clings
to "I" is the mind; that which clings to "other" is also the

mind. So the next question is: Where is the mind? It must be somehow in the body, because when the mind is not present, we have only a corpse. So ask yourself, is it in the top part of the body or the lower part? How big is it? What color is it? If you pull a hair out of your head, it hurts, doesn't it? If you prick your foot on a thorn, it hurts, doesn't it? The mind and body must be somehow coextensive, mustn't they? It's as though the mind and body were stuck to each other. On the other hand, when someone is killed in an accident, where does the mind go? How did it leave the body and from where? It's only when we examine the mind correctly that we discover how many false assumptions we have—false assumptions that, for the moment, are completely unnoticed. We cling to things as though they were permanent and will last forever. This is the measure of our delusion, tightly fettered as we are by this so-called "I" of ours—this "I," in the interests of which, our mind enslaves our body and our speech, and creates all sorts of difficulties and hardships.

When we arrive at a correct understanding of the mind, we can see that our present thoughts are just like waves on the water. At one moment they arise; at another they dissolve. And that's all there is to it: the mind is nothing but thoughts. The mind, which is empty, arises as thought, and this is also empty. The stream of consciousness, which is empty, is carried away by thoughts that are likewise empty. This is how the mind falls and remains in the six realms of samsara. It is the mind itself that fabricates samsara, and it does so because it fails to recognize its own nature.

Now that we have some idea of the mind's nature and how it works, we must bring it under control and master it. In order to do this, it is said that that we must keep our body perfectly still. Moreover, if the body is straight, the subtle channels will be straight. If the subtle channels are straight, the wind-energy will be unobstructed. And if the wind-energy is unobstructed, the mind will rest in its natural, unaltered flow.[7] Therefore, keep your body still and reduce your speech to a minimum. Don't think about what you have just been doing. Don't think about what you are going to do later. Without concern for the past or the future, let your mind rest in its natural state. This state, in which the mind is left as it is, untampered with and natural, is called "rest" or "stillness." This "stillness" is actually just the mind itself. You could call it the "mind of the present moment," or the "awareness of the present moment." But whatever you call it, it is what—in this very moment—is actually knowing and joyfully aware.

A mind that is not agitated by thoughts concerning the past, present, and future, a mind that is thought-free, is a state that is stunningly vast and open. It is full of joy. Even when the mind's nature is recognized, it is impossible to describe. It is empty. It rests in awareness. But this resting in the radiance of awareness does not last long. There is nothing permanent about it, for thoughts will certainly arise, strong and clear.

We talk about "arising" because thoughts flash into appearance like lightning in the sky, or swell like waves on the ocean. They are in constant movement. At the outset, thoughts appear and disappear in endless continuity. So, when beginners like us meditate, we must recognize thoughts as they arise. If we fail to recognize them, their movement continues unnoticed below the surface and we are carried away by them. Meditating like this is of no help to us.

If you are able to continue meditating properly, certain signs will appear. For instance, some people experience a kind of physical well-being. Others, because of the particular disposition of their subtle channels and energies, experience a powerful sense of bliss. For others, it is more like a deep sleep or an all-engulfing darkness. Whether you experience bliss or clarity, avoid any kind of expectation. Do not think to yourself, "Oh, my meditation is working. I'm making progress. If only I could have more of these experiences!" On the other hand, if you experience a kind of darkness, a thoughtless blankness, clear it away over and over again. If you don't, your meditation will sink slightly. Some people have lots of thoughts when they meditate—an unstoppable flood. If this happens to you, don't get upset and think that your meditation is a failure. It is just a sign that you are becoming aware of all the thoughts that under ordinary circumstances pass unnoticed. So don't let it bother you. Don't think you have to suppress or eliminate your thoughts. Whatever happens, it is said that you must meditate without hope or fear, doubt or expectation. That's the main thing.

It is thanks to the blessings of the Lama that realization will dawn. Therefore pray to him, mingling your mind with his. If you do, there will come a moment when you will see that what is called the Buddha is not different from your own awareness, and that there is nothing to subdue or master other than your own thoughts. The sign that your meditation has hit the mark is that your devotion to the Lama will deepen and your compassion for beings will gain in strength. You will be your own witness and you will gain great confidence in the practice.

If you gain control over your mind, then even if you are at the point of death, you will understand that it is only because of a particular thought that there is an impression of dying–but that the nature of the mind is utterly beyond both birth and death. It would be excellent if you could gain this confidence.

So keep this little, essential, instruction in your hearts. This conviction and confidence is what we call the Dharma–the inner qualities that you gain. If you vacillate and think of Dharma as something extraneous to you, thought up by somebody else, you will not benefit from it.[8] Instead, do yourself a favor and get out of samsara! Be convinced that your mind must separate from samsara, with its karma and defilements. If you do, everything will be fine. Please practice. Pray constantly that you will have no obstacles on your path and that you might be able to capture, in this very life, the primordial citadel.[9] And I will add my prayers to yours.

THE ESSENCE 2
OF THE PATH

To my Lord of Dharma, peerless, kind,
My glorious Lama, homage!
His lotus feet I place
Upon my chakra of great bliss.

Here is my advice,
Some counsel useful for your mind.

Not to keep yourself from evil actions
Is to have no *pratimoksha*.
Not to work for others' welfare
Is to have no bodhichitta.
Not to master pure perception
Is to have no Secret Mantra.
If illusions don't collapse,
There is no realization.

If you opt for one side or the other,
That is not the View.
If you have a goal in mind,
That is not the Meditation.
If your conduct's a contrivance,
That is not the Action.
If you hope and wish,
You'll have no Fruit.

Those with faith will go for refuge;
Those who have compassion will have bodhichitta;
Those with wisdom will gain realization;
Those who have devotion harvest blessings.

Those who have a sense of shame are careful how they
    act;
Careful in their actions, they are self-possessed;
Self-possessed, they keep their vows and pledges;
Keeping vows and pledges, they will have
    accomplishment.

Peaceful self-control: the sign of one who's heard the
    teachings!
Few defiled emotions are the mark of one who
    meditates.
Harmony with others is the sign of one who practices.

A blissful heart is witness to accomplishment.
The root of Dharma is your very mind.
Tame it and you're practicing the Dharma.
To practice Dharma is to tame your mind—
And when you tame it, then you will be free!

THE LONG ORAL LINEAGE 3
OF THE NYINGMAPAS

A Teaching Given by Kyabje Dudjom Rinpoche at the
Dharma Center of Kalimpong When Bestowing the
Transmission of the Cycle of the Nyingma Kahma,
Early December 1962[10]

My dear Dharma friends, I would like to give you a short historical outline describing the main features of the cycle of the Nyingma Kahma,[11] the teachings belonging to the long lineage of oral transmission. The question has been asked recently whether the kahma teachings are the same as the Kagyupa teachings. This is not at all the case. In general, the terms *Nyingma* and *Sarma*, *old* and *new*, are used with reference to the earlier and later translations of the sacred Dharma, and only in the context of Tibetan Buddhism.[12] From the point of view of Indian Buddhism, they have no meaning.

The Buddha's doctrine was first disseminated in Tibet during the reign of King Trisong Detsen and his sons. At that time, the great Indian pandita and abbot Shantarakshita, the great master Padmasambhava, the great pandita Vimalamitra, and others, as well as the translators Vairotsana, Kawa Peltsek, Chokro Lui Gyaltsen, Ma Rinchen Chok, Nyak Jñana Kumara, and the rest—a hundred panditas and translators in all—met together and translated many texts of both sutra and tantra. These texts were definitively checked and ratified by exegesis, study, meditation, and practice, and came to be referred to as Nyingma, the "old translations."[13]

Subsequently, these teachings were suppressed by Langdarma, and Tibet was annihilated as a land of Dharma. In the western province of Ngari, however, the royal lineage survived, and during the reigns of the lama-king Yeshe Ö and his brother, the work of translating Buddhist texts was begun again by Rinchen Zangpo and others.[14] All the translations made during and after that period are referred to as Sarma—the "new translations."

Nowadays it seems that some people are saying that the Nyingmapas have no sutra teachings, and the Sarmapas are without the tantra. Such people have no learning and are ignorant of the Dharma. The Nyingmapas and the Sarmapas both possess the complete path of the sutras and tantras. In recent times also, some people, claiming to be erudite but with evil intentions, have been saying that the present Nyingma teachings have no authentic origins. They say that the Dharma had completely degenerated by the time of Langdarma, and that the *kahma* and *terma* teachings as they exist today are just our own invention. As a result, certain unlearned, weak-minded people have been led into doubt, thinking that such rumors might be true. The real situation, however, is quite different.

When Langdarma attempted to destroy the teachings, he completely suppressed the monastic order. He was unable, however, to harm the tantric lay practitioners, for he was afraid of the power of the great yogi Nubchen Sangye Yeshe.[15] The yogis were also protected by the fact that they did not have the outer distinguishing marks of the ordained sangha, and obviously no one was in a position to know that they were vessels of the Dharma, holding it within their minds. So it was that the white-robed lay *tantrikas* perfectly preserved the texts of both the sutras and the tantras, upholding them through exegesis, study, meditation, and practice. It was by this means that they succeeded in keeping the Secret Mantra alive. Thanks to their kindness, these teachings, which are like a wish-fulfilling jewel, exist to this day, and can still be found and practiced.

While Langdarma was pursuing his work of destruction, three disciples of the great abbot Shantarakshita, namely Mar, Yo, and Tsang, escaped to Kham in eastern Tibet. Following Langdarma's death, it was they who bestowed monastic ordination on Lachen Gongpa Rabsel and ten other men from the provinces of Ü and Tsang. This marks the beginning of the later spread of the Dharma in Tibet. Not long after, the great translator Rinchen Zangpo appeared and gradually there followed all the other translators of the Sarma, or new tradition. The Kadampa, Sakyapa, Kagyupa, and other transmission lineages slowly spread.[16] Following the Kadampas, the Lord Tsongkhapa founded the tradition of Riwo Ganden, or Gelugpa. Starting from the second half of the reign of the lama-king Yeshe Ö, the line of Nyingma tertöns, or treasure discoverers, began to appear.[17]

Our Nyingma teachings may be divided into the kahma teachings of the long oral lineage and the terma, or treasure texts, of the short lineage. The kahma embodies the teachings that have been transmitted from mouth to ear, from Samantabhadra right down to our present root teachers, without interruption. Within this cycle, the principal teachings[18] are the *mahayoga* tantra, *The Phantasmagorical Net*; the *anuyoga* tantra, *The Essential Compilation*; and the *atiyoga* teachings, which correspond to the tantras, their commentaries, and the essential instructions.[19] The printed canon of Nyingma tantras contains over 440 different texts.[20] There exists an enormous number of other tantras that are not included in this printed collection.

In addition to this, Guru Rinpoche lovingly devised a

sustaining remedy for the doctrine and beings living in the decadent, evil times of later centuries. He concealed wonderful treasures of teaching, together with riches and samaya substances in the snow mountains, rocks, and lakes. As time unfolds and when the moment is ripe, treasure discoverers, who are emanations of Guru Rinpoche's realized disciples, open up the hidden treasures and disseminate the teachings contained therein. These teachings constitute what we refer to as the short lineage of terma. Its principal subjects are the sadhanas of the Eight Great Herukas,[21] the *Embodiment of Wisdom*,[22] and the sadhanas of Vajrakila.[23] These comprise the various practices of the creation and perfection stages, yogic activities, rituals, and pith instructions. Up to the present time, hundreds of great tertöns have appeared, as well as over a thousand lesser ones.

On the sutra level, the kahma cycle contains teachings on pratimoksha and bodhichitta. On the tantra level, it contains teachings on the *kriya*, *upa*, and *yoga* tantras. Its principal contents, however, are the unsurpassable tantras, which, in the Nyingma system, are divided into three inner classes. As already indicated, the first class is the mahayoga (in other words, the tantra section), which includes the general tantra entitled *The Phantasmagorical Net*[24] and so forth, as well as the various mandalas related to the particular tantras of the enlightened body, speech, mind, qualities, and activities. The second class is the anuyoga (that is, the section of esoteric teachings on the tantra), with the mandala of *The United Assembly*[25] connected with the nine gradual vehicles. The third is the atiyoga (that is, the section of essential instructions). This is further divided into (a) the outer cycle on the mind, comprising eighteen tantras;[26] (b) the inner cycle on the vast expanse, consisting of *The Bridge of Diamond*[27] and other tantras; and (c) the secret cycle, which consists of the seventeen tantras[28] and many other texts.

A study of the various Nyingma histories of the Dharma shows that the kahma teachings are the very foundation of the Nyingma tradition as it was previously propagated in Tibet, and demonstrates the greatness of its lineage holders. The tradition of the *Phantasmagorical Net*, in other words, the *Guhyagarbha-tantra* and so forth, and the exegesis and practical instructions for these teachings, have been preserved unspoiled until the present day by the majority of the Nyingma monasteries. These are the foundations of Dorje Drak and Mindroling in central Tibet, Kathog and Pelyul in lower Kham, and Shechen and Dzogchen in the middle region.

But in our day, armies of barbarians, fired by dreadful, evil intentions, have attacked and annihilated the teachings, the monasteries, and the sangha that upheld the doctrine in both central Tibet and Kham. Not even a single text was spared. This is the terrible calamity that has befallen us. Despite everything, however, and after all the fighting in Tibet, I worked very hard to bring to India all the books that belonged to me in Pemakö.

Now, Zhadeu Trulshik Rinpoche (who feels a great responsibility for the continuation and preservation of the teachings) often said to me that he wished to receive the explanation and transmission of the entire range of empowerments and transmissions of the kahma teachings. At the cost of great physical hardship, he recently journeyed here from Solu-Khumbu, bringing offerings, in order to repeat his request. Thus, even now, it is still possible to teach and propagate the empowerments and transmissions of the long oral lineage of kahma. It shows that, even in these days of great darkness, the lifeline and continuity of our teachings have not necessarily been severed. This is something we should be happy about.

Years ago, when I was twenty, I was at Mindroling monastery and received many empowerments, instructions, and transmissions belonging to this cycle of the kahma teachings, together with the sadhanas of the Eight Great Herukas, the *Embodiment of Wisdom*, and so forth. There were many lamas and tulkus receiving them at the same time, of whom the principal recipients were the two sons of the Mindroling lineage: Minling Khen Rinpoche Khyentse Norbu and Minling Chung Rinpoche Ngawang Chödrak.[29] However, on numerous occasions, the great abbot and *vajradhara* said, addressing himself especially to me, "I am giving you all the empowerments, transmissions, and instructions of the most important kahma and terma teachings.[30] It is now your task to uphold the doctrine of the Nyingmapas. You must keep and preserve the books of kahma and terma. You must expound and propagate them, and never miss an opportunity to do so." Now, when I think about what he said, I see that his words were prophetic.

Also, when I was receiving *The Precious Treasury of Termas*[31] from the Lord Phuktrul Rinpoche,[32] he said to me jokingly, "Of all the disciples of the two Jamgöns, Jamyang Khyentse Wangpo[33] and Jamgön Kongtrul Lodro Thaye,[34] only I have given *The Precious Treasury of Terma*s as many as five times. But you will give it ten times." I remember wondering how on earth this could be true. But I can see now that he too was speaking with clairvoyant foresight, since even though I never planned to do so, I have in fact given it nine times.[35]

Well now, I, your old father, have no qualities at all, except one. My root teachers, learned and accomplished as they were, were Padmasambhava in person. I never did a single thing to disappoint them, nothing that they could regard as even mildly inappropriate, let alone anything that went against their wishes. That's my main achievement: my samaya is undamaged. And I confess that with such a pure lineage, I do feel rather pleased with myself! It's pretty unusual these days, isn't it?

Of the two thousand or so people who are now receiving these empowerments and transmissions, there are thirty-seven tulkus and about sixty abbots, professors, and teachers. The majority are members of the monastic and tantric sanghas, practitioners of the Dharma. About a quarter of the assembly is made up of the laity, both men and women. In the past, it was not the custom to give the profound empowerments of the Secret Mantra openly to a large number of people. The only people to whom they were granted were those who would be certain to practice them and who would be able to keep the samaya.

It is said that the Vinaya should be adapted to the customs of the country in which it is being observed and I will act according to the same principle. Nowadays, even children are delighted to receive empowerments and nobody would be happy if they were turned away. Nevertheless, when people are asked whether they are able to practice or not, if they answer that they can when in fact they can't, the samaya will be spoiled. This will be a downfall both for myself and for others. On the other hand, people with wrong views do not come to receive empowerments, even if they are invited. Consequently, I shall regard all those attending as faithful disciples and will bestow empowerment on them. It is generally said, for example in the *Chandrapradipa-sutra*, that the mind of each and every being is pervaded by the sugatagarbha. This being so, no one is an improper vessel for empowerment. All should be accepted in a spirit of bodhichitta. Of course, people without understanding are naturally cut off from these great skillful means, for they are "self-secret." In view of this, I think that the fault of teaching the Secret Mantra to a large and indiscriminate crowd will not occur.

Regarding the empowerment itself, each and every word must be clearly understood, and what is to be visualized and meditated upon must be clearly present to the mind. If this is not the case, and there is no understanding of what is taking place, it is impossible to say that the mere touching of the head with the empowerment substances or tasting the water from the vase will result in the maturation of the mind. All the same, the root of the Secret Mantra is pure perception. If one has pure perception and devotion free from doubt, if one can consider the Lama as the true manifestation of the main deity in the mandala and look upon the empowerment substances as true *amrita*, blessed by him, it is said that the mere sight of the mandala of the Secret Mantra, or the mere hearing of the name of the yidam deity, will be a source of immeasurable benefits. In such cases, it is certain that the blessing of the empowerment is transmitted.

Once one has received an empowerment, it is essential to observe the samaya. This is like putting a snake inside a bamboo cane. The snake can go either up or down; there is no side exit in the middle. In other words, if you do not damage the samaya, you will go straight up to the buddhafields; if you damage it, you will go straight down to the hell realms. It is vital to appreciate the importance of observing the samaya and of putting the teachings into practice. You must do this for your own sake. And there are many different samayas to be observed, many teachings to be practiced. You must know how to observe them all, condensing them into a single essence.

There is no greater fault for Dharma practitioners than to practice the Dharma incorrectly. Motivation and practice should never be at cross-purposes. This is crucial. Don't be hypocritical. It won't do just to mouth formulas like "I take refuge, I take refuge" and "*Nyingje, nyingje*—beings are suffering. Oh, how sad!" while at the same time you neglect such things as faith, samaya, and the karmic law of cause and effect, running after your selfish aims in a completely two-faced way.

The authentic Buddhadharma is not something outside the mind. It dwells within. This is why Buddha has said:

> Abandon every evil deed,
> Practice virtue well,
> Perfectly subdue your mind:
> This is Buddha's teaching.

If we condense this verse into a single point, it means that every action, whether great or small, that is motivated by the three poisons of craving, aversion, and ignorance, is negative. This is what we must strive to eliminate. If we completely give up harming others and eradicate the negative intentions that are the root of this, the pratimoksha vows will be perfectly observed. Again, all actions, big or small, that are not defiled by the three poisons are positive. This is what we must accomplish. If we are not stained by the three poisons, we will gradually acquire the altruistic attitude of wishing to benefit others. The whole of bodhichitta is complete in this altruistic attitude and the activities that bring benefit to others. It is through virtuous or nonvirtuous intentions that negative and positive actions are perpetrated. The source of all virtue and nonvirtue is thus the mind alone, and it is over our minds that we must mount an unceasing guard. All the eighty-four thousand teachings of the Buddhadharma were set forth for one reason only: to tame the mind. If we succeed in bringing our wild, rough minds to heel, all ordinary perceptions and clingings will naturally dissolve, and the "infinite purity" of all phenomena will become manifest.³⁶ In this way, the samayas of the Secret Mantra are complete and perfect.

Subduing the mind leads naturally to the development of a good heart. This is what we are referring to when we use the beautiful word *bodhichitta*. Furthermore, the samayas of the Secret Mantra relate not to the actions of body and speech (which are the specific preserve of the Vinaya) but to the mind. And they can be damaged in a single instant. For example, as soon as you feel strong and genuine hatred toward one of the Dharma kindred, you have committed the third downfall of the Vajrayana.[37] If you have genuine contempt for a non-Buddhist religion (to say nothing of other Buddhist tenet systems), you have committed the sixth downfall. You must repair your samaya as soon as it is damaged. The more you delay, the heavier the fault will be. Consequently, if you commit even a small infraction or allow the samaya to degenerate even slightly, do not dismiss it as unimportant but diligently confess it at once.

Once you have received the empowerment of any deity of the three roots, you are bound from then on to consider the yoga related to the body, speech, and mind of that deity as your essential meditation.[38] This is your samaya. Of course, you may not be able to perform lots of meditations and recitations on all sorts of deities, but if you meditate on Vajrasattva, the sovereign of all mandalas, you will in fact be meditating on all of them. This meditation is praised as a way of purifying all breaches, downfalls, and negativities. It is very important to make an effort and recite the hundred-syllable mantra at least twenty-one times daily, within the framework of a confession practice. To sum up, if you are able to extract the essence of the empowerment you have received by maintaining a virtuous lifestyle and a good meditation practice, you yourself are the one who will benefit.

Here we all are. Despite the fact that no announcement was made that these empowerments were to take place, we have managed to come together, drawn by our past pure connections with the Dharma, our karma, and our aspirations. If we continue to pray and make the repeated aspiration to meet again in the buddhafields in our next lives, I am sure that this will happen.

I therefore request you all, masters and disciples, to have the utterly pure attitude of bodhichitta. Aspire constantly and pray without ceasing that this precious Buddha-dharma, the source of every prosperity and joy, should prevail and spread. Pray that His Holiness the Dalai Lama, the head and crown jewel, the supreme protector of the snowy land, together with all the great holders of the doctrine, should live long and that their activities may constantly increase. Pray too that all the beings in the world, particularly of this noble land of India, and especially of Tibet, the Land of Snow, be swiftly freed from the suffering and torment inflicted in this decadent age, and that they be set before a feast of fresh and perfect happiness and prosperity.

Lamas and tulkus, there is just one last thing. I want to tell you of my great hope and expectation. I am an old man, and my health is not so good. In any case, it will be hard for me to continue to teach and spread the empowerments and transmissions of the kahma teachings to any great extent. But now I have been able to give them to you in their entirety, and this has made me very happy. You have inherited the riches of your forefathers, and you must not allow these profound instructions, which are like wish-fulfilling jewels, to decline. This is the great responsibility that you must feel.

All the scriptures of the Nyingma kahma were completely destroyed, except for this one set of mine. If one single folio is lost from it, the cycle in its entirety will be destroyed. So I request you, lamas and tulkus, to copy and publish these books as much as possible. Practice and accomplish them for your own sake and for the sake of others. Teach them. Propagate them, so that the stream of the teachings is not severed but remains forever. Give the greatest attention to upholding and preserving the teachings. This is of the utmost importance, and from my heart, I entreat you.

P RACTICING 4
THE TEACHINGS
WITHOUT SECTARIAN BIAS

*A Discourse on the Importance of Practicing with Trust and
Devotion the Teachings to which One Feels Drawn* [39]

I would like to say a few things to you, my vajra brothers
and sisters, gathered here. We Tibetans are from a country
where the Buddha's teaching was deeply rooted. It may
indeed be said that we were born in the buddhafield of
the noble Avalokiteshvara, and we all understand, more or
less, what is meant by Dharma. However, the factor that
differentiates Buddhists from non-Buddhists is taking refuge in the Three Jewels of Buddha, Dharma, and Sangha.
Those who take refuge are Buddhists; those who do not
are non-Buddhists. Of the Three Jewels, the Buddha revealed the sunlight of the sacred teachings in the dark

abyss of this world. He is our guide and benefactor, and indeed that of all living beings. He set forth inconceivable teachings of the supreme Dharma in order to lead us to the buddhafields and to liberation. The Dharma is our path. Those who uphold the Dharma by listening to it, teaching it, and practicing it are called the Sangha. These Three Jewels possess extraordinary qualities, and it is thanks to them that liberation from the suffering of samsara and the lower destinies, and the attainment of the everlasting joy of buddhahood, are possible. We must recognize what the Three Jewels are and take refuge in them.

We become Buddhists by taking refuge. Now, the root, the factor that brings us to take refuge, is faith, and this, therefore, is the very foundation of Dharma. At the outset, faith and devotion are what impel us to take refuge; they enable us to assimilate it and make it part of ourselves. If there is no faith, there is no refuge, and without refuge, we cannot absorb the blessings of the Three Jewels. Therefore, with sincere trust in the Three Jewels, and with confidence that they are our unfailing and constant guardians, we should seek their protection, relying on them totally. This is what taking refuge means. Our faith should be as solid and unwavering as a mountain, as unfathomable and boundless as the sea. It should be constant. If it is unstable and we have only the appearance of faith, if we "take refuge" only when everything is going well and we feel fine, it will be hard for the blessings of the Three Jewels to penetrate our being.

Taken as a whole, this world is a place where the doctrine of the Buddha Shakyamuni has appeared, together with the Secret Mantra teachings, the Vajrayana. Especially in the snowy land of Tibet, thanks to the compassion of all the buddhas and the cooperative merit of beings, the teachings of both the sutras and the tantras appeared together, like the sun rising in the sky. Since we are by temperament drawn to the Mahayana, we understand that there is not one of the infinite multitude of beings throughout the vast reaches of space that has not been our father or mother. And we acknowledge that at one moment or another, they have all taken great care of us, just like our parents in this present life. We therefore feel responsible for them all—these parents of ours—and when we recite even a single mani, we do it for their sake. When we perform even a single prostration, we do it for them. This is the attitude and motivation of the Mahayana.

We may understand that we have fallen into the mire of samsara and the lower realms. But if our wish is to gain liberation only for ourselves, if we lack this altruistic attitude of wanting to bring happiness to others, our orientation will be that of the Hinayana, not the Mahayana. Even if we take refuge wishing to gain liberation, our limited attitude will result only in the ability to traverse the paths of the shravakas and pratyekabuddhas.

Taking refuge and cultivating bodhichitta—the decision to attain enlightenment for the sake of all beings—are the preliminary groundwork for all practices. Whatever practice we do derives from the Buddha's teaching, the union of the sutras and tantras. Thanks to our stock of merit, the Buddhadharma came to Tibet. Appearing first during the reign of the religious king Songtsen Gampo, it was definitively established at the time of the abbot Shantarakshita, the master Padmasambhava, and the religious king Trisong Detsen.[40] And it has remained until the present day without degeneration or decline. As a result, and also because the Dharma contains a wealth of instructions suited to the various needs of beings, a whole range of doctrinal teaching appeared in our country. Because the texts were rendered from Sanskrit into Tibetan at different times, we speak of the old translations and the new translations. Within these two categories, there are many subschools, but they are all essentially the same. They are all the teachings of the Buddha. They are all the immaculate words of Buddha himself. Therefore all the different schools, whether they derive from the earlier or later periods of translation, such as the Nyingma, Kagyu, Sakya, or Gelug, are really different only in name. In their essence they are all a single doctrine: the word of the Buddha. This means that although we should follow the tradition to which we feel drawn, we should never presume to criticize other schools. If we train in our own tradition with faith and devotion, it is certain that we are following the unmistaken path of the Buddhadharma. If, by contrast, we practice with partiality and a sense of sectarian difference, believing that our own practice is the only right one, and if we denigrate the other teachings, we are committing a very serious fault. The Buddha said that only he and those on his level could be the judge of others. No one else. Therefore, since emanations of the buddhas and bodhisattvas are everywhere, do not criticize others. Instead, train in pure perception and practice the teachings to which you aspire.

Pursuing this same theme, we can say that a particularity of us Tibetans is that not one of us, not even a single child, is ignorant of the mani. There is not one of us who lacks faith in the Dharma. It would be unimaginable. Of course, we are now only refugees, but when we escaped, we had—and still have—the Three Jewels in our hearts. We did not leave them behind. We should practice with a one-pointed confidence in them, bringing all the multitude of Buddha's teachings into a single essence. After all, it is impossible to practice all the teachings separately. Nobody can do that, or even knows how! So the question is how to condense all these teachings and practices into one. Lord Buddha has said: Abandon every evil deed, practice virtue well, perfectly subdue your mind. This is Buddha's teaching.

What is evil? What is negativity? Evil is action that harms others. Moreover, it is said that not only should we refrain from harming others in the present, we should refrain from doing things to harm ourselves in the future (as the result of evil karma). Again, what is virtue? It is the good heart, the wish to benefit others. This is what we call bodhichitta. If we have a good heart, wishing the welfare of others, and if we bring benefit to others and to ourselves, we are practicing virtue. Virtue depends exclusively on a good heart. We may well recite the refuge prayer, but if we harbor evil thoughts, it is meaningless. As the saying goes, "With good motivation, all the grounds and paths are excellent. With evil motivation, all the grounds and paths are ruined."[41] A good motivation, a good heart—this is what we must have at all times. *This* is the Dharma and nothing else. It is not something grandiose or elaborate.

To illustrate this truth, there is a story about three men who all attained buddhahood thanks to a single clay *tsatsa*.[42] One man made the tsatsa with great devotion and faith in the Three Jewels. Later, another man found it by the roadside. He reasoned that if it were left there unprotected, the rain would damage it. Since he had nothing better to cover it with, he took off his own boot and placed it over the tsatsa. A third man found the tsatsa thus covered, and was shocked, thinking that to put a shoe on a tsatsa was disrespectful and the wrong thing to do. He therefore removed the boot. Of course, it is not right to cover a tsatsa with a shoe, but since the intention of the second man was sincere and good, and since he had perfect confidence in the Three Jewels, his act was positive. All three men are said to have attained enlightenment.

The Buddha said that we should completely subdue our minds. Whatever we do, for good or ill, it is our mind that is the true agent. In the very depths of our being, we all desire one thing: we want to be happy. We don't want to suffer. But because of this—this wanting—the three defilements of craving, aversion, and ignorance arise, and suffering is what we get. It is because of these defilements that we accumulate actions that prevent us from escaping from samsara. So it is important right from the start to see the difference between a good motivation and an evil one. Our own mindfulness should be our teacher. We must examine what is positive and what is negative with mindfulness. If positive thoughts arise, we should go along with them. If nonvirtuous thoughts arise, we should put a stop to them. A virtuous mind is the source of happiness. An unvirtuous mind is the source of pain. It's as simple as that—as we can see from our own experience. When the Buddha spoke about the hell realms and the *pretas*, he wasn't making it up. He was simply talking about how things are.[43]

Furthermore, all objects to which we show respect and make offerings are simply supports with which we practice Dharma.[44] But the Dharma itself is in our own minds. It is not something outside. It depends entirely on our good or evil intentions. So it's very important always to have a good heart. If we do, this itself means that we possess the Buddha's teaching. If we practice virtue properly, if we reject evil, if we have confidence in the karmic law of cause and effect, and if we have real trust in the Three Jewels, we will never do anything to be ashamed of. It is important not to do things that we will regret in the future.

Because of the places where we live these days, we are constantly in contact with foreigners. Our young people are falling under their influence and are losing their faith. There is a risk that they will lose interest in the Dharma. We should think about this carefully and try to find ways that this can be avoided. Never give up the Three Jewels!

Guru Rinpoche prophesied the calamity that has befallen Tibet, and he also spoke of ways it could have been avoided. From the time of the fifth[45] to the thirteenth[46] Dalai Lamas, all the ceremonies needed to avert the disaster were performed properly. But when the thirteenth Dalai Lama passed away, the prophecies were put aside and neglected, and the ceremonies and rituals were not performed as they should have been. Because of this, the prediction was fulfilled, "Evil doctrines will spread, evil forces will arise within and the people's minds will be possessed by demons." If Guru Rinpoche had been able to

perform the exorcism three times when he was in Tibet,
binding the evil forces under oath, Buddhadharma would
have remained for a very long time. But he was hindered
by wicked ministers and could only perform the exorcism
twice.[47] This is why our country has sunk into the catastro-
phe that you know only too well.

And yet, in the midst of this terrible situation, there is
at least one good thing: His Holiness the Dalai Lama.
Outwardly, he is like an iron fence and inwardly like a
precious treasure. He is our refuge in this and future lives,
the guide of gods and men. He has been able to come and
settle, without any danger to his life, in India, the noble
land. To the eye of an impartial observer, it is thanks to
this that an amazing development has taken place, both for
the Dharma and in the political situation of us Tibetans.
You all know this—you don't need me to tell you. It has all
happened thanks to His Holiness the Dalai Lama, and to
him alone. We should be endlessly grateful to him and
pray for his long life. This is vital.

But what does this imply? There is not one person
among us who has not received teachings and empowerments from His Holiness. Since we are now linked with
him in the Dharma, we must observe the samaya. If we go
around devotedly saying, "Oh, Gyalwa Rinpoche, Gyalwa
Rinpoche!"[48] but behave in a way that contradicts this
devotion, our conduct is absolutely wrong. We must act
according to His Holiness's wishes. Condensing our sa-

mayas into a single point, we must understand that we are all the disciples of the Buddha and all followers of the one teaching that is his. On this basis we should practice the tradition to which we are drawn. We must refrain from criticizing other traditions and schools, and stop entertaining wrong notions about them. We are in a foreign country; we should not make an exhibition of our bad behavior! Even if we are unable to have pure vision regarding each other, we should at the very least aim and aspire not to criticize and have wrong views about each other. Sometimes it appears we are completely at loggerheads! As soon as one problem is solved, another one arises. It's quite uncanny! So do your best to avoid such things. Older people should advise the young, and we should all raise our spirits and aspirations. This is so important at the present time. And indeed, this is the best way to pray for the long life of His Holiness and perform a real service for the Dharma.

Whether we come from this region or from farther afield, we all want Tibet to be free. We are like people gasping with thirst. To that end, laity and religious must all be truly united. And this should not be mere lip service; we must really be united like water mixed with milk. If we succeed in this, I am convinced that thanks to bodhichitta, to the unflinching resolve of the teacher, the Three Jewels, and above all, His Holiness the Dalai Lama, Tibet will once again regain its freedom. But if we fight among ourselves and constantly create difficulties for each other, this is not only a disgrace but constitutes a real obstacle. So keep this in mind, all of you. I beg you to strive to make His Holiness's wishes come true! This is my advice to you, the advice of an old man. It is indeed my testament.

A N I N T R O D U C T I O N 5
T O T H E B A R D O

*A Talk Given on the Occasion of the Empowerment of the
Thousand Buddhas Associated with the Sadhana of the
Noble Compassionate One, the Lord of Space*

It has been said that the whole of the Buddha's doctrine
could be summarized in the teaching on the six *bardos*.
The Buddhadharma is vast and profound, and the many
approaches of the various vehicles and cycles of teaching
comprise an inconceivable wealth of instruction. For those
who wish to attain the primordial citadel of buddhahood
in the course of a single human life, the practice of these
teachings is presented within the framework of the six
bardos.

What, therefore, is a bardo? A bardo is a state that is
"neither here nor there"; by definition it is something that
comes "in between," an intermediate state. The six bardos

are: (1) the natural bardo of the present life; (2) the hallucinatory bardo of dreaming; (3) the bardo of meditative absorption; (4) the painful bardo of dying; (5) the luminous bardo of ultimate reality; and (6) the karmic bardo of becoming.

1. THE NATURAL BARDO OF THE PRESENT LIFE

The natural bardo of the present life covers the period between birth and death. At this moment, therefore, we are all in the bardo of the present life. As it is said in the teachings, "*Kyema!* Now that I am in the bardo of my life, I will stop being lazy, for in this life, there is no time to spare!" This is our present condition. We should think carefully and ask ourselves how many years have already gone by since we were born. How many years are still to go? Life is utterly impermanent; nothing and no one can escape death. It is impossible for any of us to stay forever. While we are in this situation, we squander our existence meaninglessly, throwing away our time in laziness and distractions. Life runs its course, and its impetus is eventually exhausted. At that point all activities are terminated, and nothing further can be done.

This is why it is said that we should not allow ourselves to fall under the power of indolence and distraction. We should instead practice the Dharma, the one thing that will help us at the time of death. Although we are unable to practice everything, we should practice as much as we can, knowing that it is by the way we live now that we can exert a positive influence on the conditions of the life to come. As much as possible, therefore, we should avoid even a single negative deed and never miss the opportunity of performing even the slightest positive action. For nothing is certain; and it is said that we should conduct ourselves so that we have nothing to regret, even if we were to die tomorrow. This, then, is the first bardo, the bardo of the present life.

2. THE HALLUCINATORY BARDO OF DREAMING
The bardo of the dream state covers the period from the moment we fall asleep till the moment we wake up the following morning. This period is similar to death; temporal duration is the only difference. During sleep, the five perceptions of form, sound, smell, taste, and contact are withdrawn into the alaya. They faint into it, so to speak, and in fact, falling asleep is actually like dying. To begin with, no dreams appear; there is only a black darkness as the sleeping person sinks unconscious into the alaya.

Later, the patterns of clinging and perception reassert themselves, stimulated by the karmic energy of ignorance.[49] As a result of this, the "sense-objects" (form, sound, smell, taste, and contact) manifest once again in the dream state. These appearances, these dream-objects, are not, of course, actually present inside oneself. On the other hand, the consciousness does not move outward toward external things. It remains within and its perceptions are imaginary and deluded. This is why this state is called the bardo of hallucination. In the nocturnal dream state, perception is subject to delusion, as it is during the day. The deluded consciousness wanders through forms, sounds, smells, tastes, and contact—all the perceptions experienced during the day, except that now they are even more hallucinatory. As the sleeper dreams, he or she sees only delusions and figments.

In fact, the teachings say that we are also like illusions and dreams ourselves. Of course, we think that a dream is something unreal when compared with waking life, which we regard as true. For buddhas, however, dreams and the perceptions of the waking state are on an equal footing. Neither corresponds to reality. They are both false: fluctuating, impermanent, deceptive—and nothing else. If we look for all the things we have done and experienced from the time of our birth until the present, where are they? There is nothing to be found. Everything goes; everything is in constant flux. This is obviously true, and yet it is something that habitually escapes us. We constantly relate to our perceptions as if they were permanent realities, thinking, "This is me, this is mine." But the teachings tell us that this is all a mistake, and is the very thing that causes us to wander in samsara.

Come what may, it is our hallucinatory (dream) perceptions that we have to work with. During the day, we should pray to the Lama and the Three Jewels, and at night we should strive to recognize our dreams as the delusions they are. We have to be able to transform our dreams; we must practice the Dharma even while dreaming. We need to gain proficiency in this, because if we succeed, we will be able to mingle our daytime perceptions with our dream perceptions without drawing a distinction between them, and our practice will be greatly enhanced. The teachings specify that this practice is an extremely effective way of dealing with the fact of impermanence, and with every other obstacle as well.

3. The Bardo of Meditative Absorption

The bardo of meditative absorption may be described as the period of time we spend in meditative equipoise. It terminates when we arise from this state. It is called a bardo because it is not like our ordinary current of deluded thoughts, nor is it like phenomenal perception as experienced in the course of life. It is a period of meditative stability, a state of concentration as fresh and untarnished as the sky. It is like a motionless ocean in which there are no waves. It is impossible to remain in this state when the mind is full of thoughts (appropriately likened to a gang of robbers), or even when it is occupied with more subtle mental undercurrents, mixed and matted together like threads. Stable meditation is impossible in such circumstances. The teachings say that meditators must not fall under the power of their thoughts, which are like thieves. They should instead have undistracted mindfulness and powerful diligence with which they can prevent their concentration from disintegrating.

The dream bardo and the bardo of meditative absorption are subdivisions of the present life. The bardo of the present life naturally includes our practice. Even if it is intermittent, it is of necessity performed within the scope of our present existence. It is only here that we can meditate.

4. THE PAINFUL BARDO OF DYING

It is perfectly possible, from one day to the next, to discover that we are suffering from a fatal illness. When all the ceremonies and prayers for long life have proved ineffective, and the approach of death is certain, it will finally dawn on us that nothing we have done in our lives has been of any use. We must leave it all behind. Even if we have a stack of wealth as high as Mount Meru, we cannot take it with us. We cannot take so much as a needle and thread! It is time for us to go; even this body that we love so much will have to be abandoned. What *can* we take with us? Only our positive and negative karma. The actions that we have stored up will be our only companions.

However, suppose we have put the instructions into practice and trained in the transference of consciousness. If we have gained proficiency in this, and if we can die without a trace of regret, we will certainly have done ourselves a very great favor. A person who says, "I shall go to such and such a buddhafield," and does in fact do so, is a perfect practitioner. Let's face it: we practice the Dharma because we need it at the moment of our death. This is why the teachings stress the importance of understanding what happens when we die.

It is said that even for an ordinary person, the moment of death is crucial. It is a moment when we should pray to the Lama and the Three Jewels. We should cut through the strings that bind us to our possessions—our house and everything else. For this is what pulls us into samsara. We should also make offerings of our wealth to the Three Jewels, praying that we will not have to go through a painful and difficult death and suffer in the lower realms afterward.

If we have successfully trained in the transference of consciousness, and if we are able to apply this technique when the moment of death arrives and thus transfer our consciousness successfully—this is surely the best situation of all. But if we can't do this, the transference of consciousness can be done for us by a lama or one of our vajra brothers or sisters who happens to be with us and knows how to do it. The consciousness should be transferred to the buddhafield as soon as respiration stops.[50] In any case, it is important to plan for this and get ourselves up to scratch, so that when the crucial moment comes, there is no need to be afraid. Needless to say, the preparation has to be done *now*, during the bardo of the present life.

What happens to us when we die? From the moment of physical conception, the moment of the union of our parents, our body begins to coalesce from the essence of the five elements.[51] It is a gathering of the elements, of warmth, energy, the subtle channels, and so forth. When we die, these five elements gradually separate and dissolve into each other. When this dissolution is complete, outer respiration stops, and the inner pulses are reabsorbed. The white essence, received from our father and located in the brain, and the red essence, received from our mother and located in the navel, meet in the heart center and mingle. Only then does the mind leave the body.

At this point, in the case of those who have no experience of the practice, the minds falls into a prolonged state of unconsciousness. But for those who are accomplished masters or experienced meditators, the consciousness will, after two minutes or so, dissolve into space, and space will dissolve into luminosity. What is the fruit of meditation for those of us who practice? It is precisely this so-called dissolution into luminosity, which is pure and untarnished like the sky. It occurs when the inner pulse stops. If a person has achieved stability in the recognition of luminosity during meditation, then as soon as the experience of untarnished space arises, there occurs the so-called meet-

ing of the mother and child luminosities, space and awareness.[52] This is liberation. At root, this is what lamas and
meditators who practice refer to as "resting in *thuktam*," or
meditation, at the time of death. Thuktam is nothing more
than this. The mother and child luminosities mingle; stability in the phases of creation and perfection is gained.
This is liberation.

5. THE LUMINOUS BARDO OF ULTIMATE REALITY
If we have not practiced, we faint when the experience of
blackness arises, only to reawaken almost immediately into
the fearful perceptions of what is referred to as the fifth
bardo, the bardo of ultimate reality.[53] At this point, the
peaceful and wrathful deities appear.[54] They are implicit
and present in our awareness, from Samantabhadra to the
buddhas of the five families and the eight manifestations
of Guru Rinpoche. Their appearance is accompanied by
startling sounds and lights. At this point, people who are
unfamiliar with the practice are terrified. As soon as their
fear overwhelms them, these manifestations of awareness
dissolve and melt away.

I would now like to say a few words about the bardo of
dying and the bardo of ultimate reality together. After
the five elements separate and dissolve, the consciousness
dissolves into space, fainting into the state of alaya. Following this, luminosity is seen. It is like pure, immaculate
space. If you have no experience of meditation, you will

fail to recognize this luminosity. Being unrecognized, it will not stay for long. If you are used to concentration, however, the two luminosities, mother and child, will mingle.

Just before you start to die, before the gradual dissolution of the elements takes place, the most important thing is to be perfectly aware that you are actually dying. You must sever all attachment to the things of this life. When death arrives, you should pray to the Three Jewels, for there is no other hope than them. You should also invoke your root teacher, for he or she is somehow more accessible to you. When all is said and done, your root teacher is their embodiment. Pray to your teacher, your very yidam deity, on the dangerous pathways of the bardo. Confess all the negative actions you have committed during your life and pray to your teacher one-pointedly, asking to be led to a buddhafield immediately after death. It is said that this kind of undistracted prayer, with this aspiration constantly present before the mind, is actually a precondition for being led to a pure field.

Furthermore, when a sick person is dying, his teacher or his Dharma kindred (whose samaya is unspoiled and with whom he has a harmonious relationship) should remind him that the elements are dissolving as it is actually happening. They should pray and chant, invoking the teacher. These aspirations—to be delivered from danger on the pathways of the bardo—will be of great help. When an invalid falls down, other people pick him up. In the same way, Dharma friends can be of help; they can guide the dying person and pray for him. This is very beneficial.

It is said that the buddhas are endowed with great compassion, and if one invokes them by name (immaculate Ratnashikhin, protector Amitabha, the Buddha Shakyamuni, and so forth), the sufferings of the lower realms are dispelled even as their names are spoken. In the same way, if the dying person is able to pray well, the buddhas prevent him from entering the path to the lower realms simply owing to the fact that their names are uttered. This therefore is most useful. Prayer is like our helper and protective escort at the time of death. It is of great importance and benefit.

First of all, the dying person faints into a blank, unconscious state. Then consciousness remanifests, the luminosity appears and, if it is not recognized, vanishes, and the visions of the bardo of ultimate reality begin to dawn. This is when the manifestations of the peaceful and wrathful deities occur, with frightening sounds and lights and the impressions of terrible chasmic precipices. If one fails to recognize that these incredible sounds and rays of light are nothing but the projections of one's own mind and nothing but the creative power of awareness, a feeling of terrible dread arises. The visions occur, fear arises, and then the visions fade away. The consciousness then leaves the body, exiting by the appropriate opening.[55]

6. THE KARMIC BARDO OF BECOMING

At this point the separation of the mind and body occurs. Since the mind is now divided from the body, it is without a physical support. The gross material body is gone, and there is only a subtle body composed of light. This subtle body lacks the essential substances received from the father and mother, and consequently the dead person has no further perception of the light of sun and moon. Nevertheless, there is a kind of luminescent glimmering, a mental energy, emitted from the light body. This creates the impression that one can see one's way. In addition, all the beings who are wandering in the bardo of becoming are able to see and hear each other. Another aspect of this bardo is that whenever the bardo consciousness wishes to be somewhere, it is instantaneously present in that very place. The only places it is barred from are the womb of its future mother and Vajrasana, the sacred place where all the buddhas attain enlightenment.[36] The bardo body is a "mental body," which is why it is present in a place as soon as that place is thought of.

The mind of a dead person also possesses a certain clairvoyance, albeit tinged with defilement. It knows what other people are thinking. A recently dead person can perceive how others are using the possessions he had accumulated in the course of his life, what they are thinking about, and how they are performing the meritorious practices for his sake. The living do not see the dead, but the dead can perceive the living. Bardo beings congregate together and suffer from the sensations of hunger and thirst, heat and cold. They experience intense suffering as they wander in the intermediate state.

Those who actually wander in the bardo are those who have failed to practice much virtue in their lives, but at the same time, have not accumulated too much evil. Beings who have committed great evil will not experience the bardo of becoming at all. As soon as they close their eyes in death, they instantly arrive in the lower realms. On the other hand, those who have accumulated great merit arrive at once in a buddhafield. In general, though, people like ourselves, who are neither great sinners nor great saints, will have to experience the bardo of becoming, and this is nothing but suffering. On the other hand, the deceased may be protected from the horrors of the bardo and attain liberation. This will happen if a person has accomplished many meritorious actions, has made offerings to the Three Jewels, has given charity to the poor, and so forth; and if others have constructed the mandala of the peaceful and wrathful deities and performed the ritual in which a piece of paper with the name of the deceased person written on it has been burned, and if empowerment has been conferred (leading the consciousness of the dead person to higher destinies). It is rather like when a crowd of people rush together to catch and save someone from falling over a precipice. This is why it is said that we should perform many virtuous actions for the sake of the dead.

During the first twenty-one days after death, the deceased have the same sort of perceptions they had during life. They have the impression of possessing the same body and mind as before, and they perceive the same surroundings they experienced during their life. Later on, they begin to have perceptions related to the place where they will take rebirth in the next life. This is why it is said that the period of forty-nine days—particularly the first three weeks—is extremely important. During that time, if a lot of merit is accumulated by others for the sake of the dead, it is said that even if the people in question should be on their way to the lower realms, the compassion of the Three Jewels can lead them to a higher destiny. After that period, however, their karma will propel them into the lower realms and, though the compassion of the Three Jewels remains unchanged, that compassion is powerless to lead them to a higher destiny until their negative karma has been exhausted.

This, then, is why it is important to accumulate a great deal of merit for the sake of the dead. Dharma people, who are used to the practice, recognize, when they are in the bardo of becoming, that they have died. They realize where they are, and they remember their teacher and their yidam deity. By praying one-pointedly to them, they are able to gain rebirth in pure lands like Sukhavati, Abhirati, or the Glorious Copper-Colored Mountain.[57]

It is also possible for an accomplished lama to summon the bardo consciousness of the deceased into their written names and then reveal the true path to them. By giving teachings and empowerment, he can show them the way to the buddhafields, or at least bring the bardo consciousness to the attainment of a human birth.[58] Everything depends on the karma, aspiration, and devotion of the deceased. Of all the bardos, the most crucial one is the bardo of the present life. For it is *now*, in the bardo of the present life, that we must act and practice well, so that we will not have to wander in the other bardos.

The *sadhana* of the Great Compassionate One is the very essence of all the sutras and the tantras. Guru Rinpoche distilled it as a method whereby disciples who have connections with it will be able to take birth in Sukhavati. He subsequently concealed it as a terma, and it was the Vidyadhara Dudul Dorje, the previous Dudjom, who revealed it.[59]

We may say that the sire and forefather of the teaching of all the buddhas is the Buddha Samantabhadra or Amitabha (who are in fact identical). Never stirring from the peaceful expanse of his mind, the Buddha Amitabha looks with unceasing compassion on all the beings of the six realms. From the radiance of his love, Avalokiteshvara, the Great Compassionate One, arises. Avalokiteshvara, or Chenrezig, is the spontaneous embodiment of the compassionate speech of all the buddhas. In the presence of Amitabha, he made the promise that until the three worlds were emptied of beings, he would refrain from entering enlightenment, and would remain a bodhisattva. He promised, in other words, that he would remain until the very depths of samsara were churned and emptied of beings. From that moment on, with great compassion he has led the beings of the three realms to Sukhavati, the pure land of Amitabha.

There is a legend that once there was a moment when he thought he had completed his task and that samsara had been emptied. But he turned around and in that instant saw that there was exactly the same number of beings—no more, no less—as there was before. Perceiving that the number of beings in samsara had not diminished, he was downcast and reflected to himself, "The time will never come when I shall have led all beings to the pure lands." Thus his pledge of bodhichitta faltered. His head burst asunder in eleven pieces and his body shattered into a thousand fragments. At that very moment, the Buddha Amitabha appeared and said:

"Son of my lineage, can it be that you have spoiled your vow of bodhichitta? Cultivate it once again and strive for the good of beings as in the past!" So saying, he blessed

Avalokiteshvara's fractured head and the thousand fragments of his body. Avalokiteshvara rose again with eleven heads and a body endowed with a thousand arms; on the hand of each arm appeared an eye. This is how Avalokita was blessed with eleven heads and a thousand arms and eyes with which to work for the sake of beings. Thanks to his enlightened aspiration, his thousand arms emanated a thousand Chakravartin kings, and from his thousand eyes appeared the thousand buddhas of this Fortunate kalpa. All of these thousand buddhas will manifest entirely through the compassion of Avalokiteshvara.

Advice for a Disciple

Namo!
Gracious Lord of all the buddha families,
The nature and embodiment of every refuge,
To you, the Lotus-Born, my jeweled crown, I bow
    in homage![60]

If I were to instruct others in the excellent way, who on earth would listen? For I am wholly without discrimination and cannot be a guide even for myself! Still, you see me with pure vision and you did ask. So rather than be a disappointment, I will say a few things as they come to mind.

All success, great and small, whether in spiritual or temporal affairs, derives from your stock of merit. So never neglect even the slightest positive deed. Just do it. In the same way, don't dismiss your little faults as unimportant— just restrain yourself! Make an effort to accumulate merit: make offerings and give to charity. Strive with a good heart to do everything that benefits others. Follow in the footsteps of the wise and carefully examine everything you do. Do not be the slave of unexamined fashions. Be sparing with your words. Be thoughtful and examine situations carefully. For the roots of discrimination must be nourished: the desire to do all that should be done and to abandon all that should be abandoned. Do not criticize the wise or be sarcastic about them. Rid yourself completely of every feeling of jealous rivalry. Do not despise the ignorant, turning away from them with haughty arrogance. Give up your pride. Give up your self-importance. All this is essential. Understand that you owe your life to the kindness of your parents, therefore do not grieve them but fulfil their wishes. Show courtesy and consideration to all who depend on you. Instill in them a sense of goodness, and instruct them to practice virtue and avoid evil. Be patient with their little shortcomings and restrain your bad temper—remember that the tiniest thing can ruin a good situation.

Do not consort with narrow-minded people, nor place your trust in new and untried companions. Make friends with honest people who are intelligent and prudent, and have a sense of propriety and courtesy. Don't keep company with bad people who care nothing about karma, those who lie and cheat and steal. Distance yourself, but do it skillfully. Do not rely on people who say sweet things to your face and do the reverse behind your back.

As for yourself, be constant amid the ebb and flow of happiness and suffering. Be friendly and even with others. Unguarded, intemperate chatter will put you in their power; excessive silence may leave them unclear as to what you mean. Keep a middle course: don't swagger with self-confidence, but don't be a doormat either. Don't run after gossip without examining the truth of it. People who know how to keep their mouths shut are rare. So don't chatter about your wishes and intentions—keep them to yourself. And whether you are speaking to an enemy, an acquaintance, or a friend, never break a confidence.

Be welcoming toward people, and smile and talk pleasantly. Keep to your position. Be respectful toward your superiors, and even when things do not go well for them, don't scorn them. At the same time, don't bow and scrape before the vulgar, even when they are proud and full of themselves.

Be skillful: do not make promises that you know you cannot keep. By the same token, honor the promises you have made, and never dismiss them as unimportant. Do not be depressed by misfortune and the failure to get what you want, instead be careful to see where your real profit and loss lie.

All such worldly conduct, adopted with proper discrimination, will result in this life's fortune and prosperity and, so it is said, a speedy passage to the divine realms.

If, however, you want to get out of samsara completely, here is some advice that should help you on your way to liberation.

If you have no contentment, you are poor no matter how much money you have. So decide that you have enough, and rid yourself of yearning and attachment. It's a rare person indeed who knows that wealth is passing and unstable, and who can practice perfect generosity. Even for those who do practice it, generosity is often soiled by the three impurities and is wasted, like good food mixed with poison.[61]

Apart from the beings agonizing in hell, there is no one in samsara who does not cherish life. Of the seven excellences of the higher realms, longevity is a karmic effect similar to its cause.[62] Therefore (if you want to have a long life) protect the lives of others. Concentrate on doing this!

Cultivate faith and devotion to the Three Jewels and to your teacher. Strive in the ten virtues and combine clear intelligence with extensive learning. Nurture a sense of personal integrity and propriety regarding others. With these seven sublime riches, you will always be happy![63]

To gain peace and happiness for oneself is the Hinayana approach of the shravakas and pratyekabuddhas. The altruism of bodhichitta is the path of beings of great potential. Therefore train yourself in the deeds of bodhisattvas, and do this on a grand scale! Shoulder the responsibility of freeing all beings from samsara. Of all the eighty-four thousand sections of the Buddha's teachings, none is more profound than bodhichitta. Make every effort on the path, uniting absolute and relative bodhichitta. This distills the essence of all the sutras and the tantras. The subduing of one's own mind is the root of Dharma. When the mind is controlled, defilements naturally subside.

Do not allow yourself to become impervious and blasé[64] regarding the Dharma; do not lead yourself astray. Let the profound Dharma sink into your mind. Now that you have obtained this excellent life, so hard to find, now that you have the freedom to practice the teachings, don't waste your time. Strive to accomplish the supreme unchanging goal. For life is passing, and there is no certainty about the time of death. Even if you should die tomorrow, you should have confidence and be without regret.

Cultivate real devotion for your root teacher, and love your vajra kindred, cultivating pure perception in their regard. Fortunate are those disciples who at all times keep their samaya and vows as dearly as their lives. They gain accomplishment quickly.

Ignorance, the five poisons, doubt, and dualistic clinging are the roots of samsara and the sufferings of the three realms. There is one antidote that removes or liberates everything in a single stroke. It is spontaneous wisdom, the primal wisdom of awareness. Be confident, therefore, in the creation stage: appearances, sounds, and thoughts are but the primordial display of deity, mantra, and primal wisdom. Then settle in the "subsequent" (anuyoga) path of the three specific perceptions, the perfection stage, the state of bliss and emptiness.[65]

Take your stand on the ultimate practice of the Heart Essence—samsara and nirvana are the display of awareness. Without distraction, without meditation, in a state of natural relaxation, constantly remain in the pure, all-penetrating nakedness of ultimate reality.

HEART JEWEL OF THE FORTUNATE

An Introduction to the Great Perfection

Homage to my teacher!
The Great Master of Oddiyana once said:
> Don't investigate the roots of things,
>   Investigate the root of Mind!
> Once the mind's root has been found,
>   You'll know one thing, yet all is thereby freed.
> But if the root of Mind you fail to find,
>   You will know everything but nothing
>   understand.

When you start to meditate on your mind, sit up with your body straight, allowing your breath to come and go naturally. Gaze into the space in front of you with eyes neither closed nor wide open. Think to yourself that for the sake of all beings who have been your mothers, you will watch awareness, the face of Samantabhadra. Pray strongly to your root teacher, who is inseparable from Padmasambhava, the Guru from Oddiyana, and then mingle your mind with his. Settle in a balanced, meditative state.

Once you are settled, however, you will not stay long in this empty, clear state of awareness. Your mind will start to move and become agitated. It will fidget and run here, there, and everywhere, like a monkey. What you are experiencing at this point is not the nature of the mind but only thoughts. If you stick with them and follow them, you will find yourself recalling all sorts of things, thinking about all sorts of needs, planning all sorts of activities. It is precisely this kind of mental activity that has hurled you into the dark ocean of samsara in the past, and there's no doubt it will do so in the future. It would be so much better if you could cut through the ever spreading, black delusion of your thoughts.

What if you are able to break out of your chain of thoughts? What is awareness like? It is empty, limpid, stunning, light, free, joyful! It is not something bounded or demarcated by its own set of attributes. There is nothing in the whole of samsara and nirvana that it does not embrace. From time without beginning, it is within us, inborn. We have never been without it, yet it is wholly outside the range of action, effort, and imagination.

But what, you will ask, is it like to recognize awareness, the face of *rigpa*? Although you experience it, you simply cannot describe it—it would be like a dumb man trying to describe his dreams! It is impossible to distinguish between yourself resting in awareness and the awareness you are experiencing. When you rest quite naturally, nakedly, in the boundless state of awareness, all those speedy, pestering thoughts that would not stay quiet even for an instant—all those memories, all those plans that cause you so much trouble—lose their power. They disappear in the spacious, cloudless sky of awareness. They shatter, collapse, vanish. All their strength is lost in awareness.

You actually have this awareness within you. It is the clear, naked wisdom of dharmakaya. But who can introduce you to it? On what should you take your stand? What should you be certain of? To begin with, it is your teacher who shows you the state of your awareness. And when you recognize it for yourself, it is then that *you are introduced to your own nature*. All the appearances of both samsara and nirvana are but the display of your own awareness; *take your stand upon awareness alone*. Just like the waves that rise up out of the sea and sink back into it, all thoughts that appear sink back into awareness. *Be certain of their disso-*

lution, and as a result you will find yourself in a state utterly devoid of both meditator and something meditated upon—completely beyond the meditating mind.

"Oh, in that case," you might think, "there's no need for meditation." Well, I can assure you that there is a need! The mere recognition of awareness will not liberate you. Throughout your lives from beginningless time, you have been enveloped in false beliefs and deluded habits. From then till now you have spent every moment as a miserable, pathetic slave of your thoughts! And when you die, it's not at all certain where you will go. You will follow your karma, and you will have to suffer. This is the reason why you must meditate, continuously preserving the state of awareness you have been introduced to. The omniscient Longchenpa has said, "You may recognize your own nature, but if you do not meditate and get used to it, you will be like a baby left on a battlefield: you'll be carried off by the enemy, the hostile army of your own thoughts!" In general terms, meditation means *becoming familiar* with the state of resting in the primordial uncontrived nature, through being spontaneously, naturally, constantly mindful. It means getting used to leaving the state of awareness alone, divested of all distraction and clinging.

How do we get used to remaining in the nature of the mind? When thoughts come while you are meditating, let them come; there's no need to regard them as your enemies. When they arise, relax in their arising. On the other hand, if they don't arise, don't be nervously wondering whether or not they will. Just rest in their absence. If big, well-defined thoughts suddenly appear during your meditation, it is easy to recognize them. But when slight, subtle movements occur, it is hard to realize that they are there until much later. This is what we call *namtok wogyu*, the undercurrent of mental wandering. This is the thief of your meditation, so it is important for you to keep a close watch. If you can be constantly mindful, both in meditation and afterward, when you are eating, sleeping, walking, or sitting, that's it—you've got it right!

The great master Guru Rinpoche has said:

A hundred things may be explained, a thousand told,
But one thing only should you grasp.
Know one thing and everything is freed—
Remain within your inner nature, your awareness!

It is also said that if you do not meditate, you will not gain certainty; if you do, you will. But what sort of certainty? If you meditate with a strong, joyful endeavor, signs will appear showing that you have become used to staying in your nature. The fierce, tight clinging that you have to dualistically experienced phenomena will gradually loosen up, and your obsession with happiness and suffering, hopes and fears, and so on, will slowly weaken. Your devotion to the teacher and your sincere trust in his instructions will grow. After a time, your tense, dualistic attitudes will evaporate and you will get to the point where gold and pebbles, food and filth, gods and demons, virtue and nonvirtue, are all the same for you—you'll be at a loss to choose between paradise and hell! But until you reach that point (while you are still caught in the experiences of dualistic perception), virtue and nonvirtue, buddhafields and hells, happiness and pain, actions and their results—all this is reality for you. As the Great Guru has said, "My view is higher than the sky, but my attention to actions and their results is finer than flour."

So don't go around claiming to be some great Dzogchen meditator when in fact you are nothing but a farting lout, stinking of alcohol and rank with lust!

It is essential for you to have a stable foundation of pure devotion and samaya, together with a strong, joyful endeavor that is well balanced, neither too tense nor too loose. If you are able to meditate, completely turning aside from the activities and concerns of this life, it is certain that you will gain the extraordinary qualities of the profound path of Dzogchen. Why wait for future lives? You can capture the primordial citadel right now, in the present.

This advice is the very blood of my heart. Hold it close and never let it go!

AN ASPIRATION TO THE 8
GREAT PERFECTION

May we gain conviction in the view
    wherein samsara and nirvana are the same.
May we have consummate skill in meditation,
    a natural flow unaltered, uncontrived.
May we bring our action to perfection,
    a natural, unintended, spontaneity.
May we find the *dharmakaya,*
    beyond all gaining and rejection.

Paris, 1976

As Told by Himself

I, Dudjom Jigdrel Yeshe Dorje, was born in the year of the wooden dragon of the fifteenth *rabjung* cycle (1904). My birthplace was the hidden land of Pemakö,[66] and my father was Jampel Norbu Wangyal of the royal line of Kanam. When I was only three years old, I was recognized by the disciples of the great tertön Dudjom Lingpa as the emanation of their master. They took me for their own, and thus I entered the door of Dharma.

"Reading and writing are the roots of knowledge," my teacher said, and he made me study hard. At the same time, I had to memorize rituals, prayers, and so forth. I received instructions on the proper conduct of body, speech, and mind. I also studied history, spiritual tales, and the preliminary practices, and thanks to this, my intelligence developed a little. As the years went by, I was compassionately guided according to my ability by learned and accomplished lamas. I studied all the basic sciences such as grammar, spelling, poetry, astrology, and medicine, as well as the Dharma texts and commentaries of Madhyamika, Prajñaparamita, the *Five Doctrines of Maitreya*, the *Bodhicharyavatara*, the *Three Vows*, and so forth. In particular, I revered the maturing and liberating tantras, their commentaries, and the profound instructions of the oral and treasure teachings of the Nyingma tradition.[67] These ranged from the thirteen great activities of a vajra master to the rituals of the various practice traditions, making and decorating *torma*s, dancing, drawing mandalas, chanting, and music. Without overlooking anything, I trained most diligently in all the practical details of the *vidyadhara* lineage. Beginning with the accumulations and trainings of the preliminaries up to the main practice, namely the approach and accomplishment sections of the creation stage, followed by the perfection stage practices, I persevered as much as I could, making up all the necessary numbers in the recitation.

However, I was led astray due to the fact that I have the unfortunate title of lama. I became a slave to the distracting activities that are said to be for the benefit of the doctrine and beings, and for that reason, I got about as much sign of accomplishment as feathers on a tortoise!

Whatever nectar of Dharma I received, most of it I explained and propagated as much as I could to others, according to their nature. And though not deserving to be numbered among the learned, yet so as not to disappoint those who requested me, and also in the hope that I might be of some service to the doctrine, I wrote and compiled more than twenty volumes. These include, for example: *The History of the Nyingma School, A General Survey of Nyingma Teachings, A History of Tibet*, a word-for-word commentary on the *Three Vows*, and instructions and guidelines for many cycles of practice. It is said that the result of receiving teaching is the ability to compose—so I wrote all these works without expectation and trepidation.

Thanks to the kindness of my great and holy teachers, the eyes of my pure perception were not blinded and I never accumulated the evil karma of abandoning the Dharma, of having wrong views and denigrating the teachings of others, or of criticizing anyone at all. I am continually training myself in the wholesome attitude of avoiding all duplicity. But as I do not have the slightest doubt that I belong among the followers of the compassionate Buddha, albeit in the lowest ranks, I do occasionally have a slight feeling of pride. Which goes to show that I can't even tell the difference between right and wrong! This is a short life story of myself, an old tantrika.

GLOSSARY

ACHARYA, Skt., *slob dpon.* Teacher, the equivalent of spiritual master or lama.

ALAYA, Skt., *kun gzhi.* Lit. the ground-of-all. This is the fundamental and indeterminate level of the mind, in which karmic imprints are stored.

AMRITA, Skt., *bdud rtsi.* Lit. the ambrosia that overcomes the "demon of death"; the draft of immortality, and symbol of wisdom.

ANUYOGA, Skt. The second of the inner classes of tantra, according to the system of nine vehicles used in the Nyingma tradition. Anuyoga emphasizes the perfection stage of tantric practice. It is typified by the wisdom of emptiness coupled with meditation on the subtle channels, energies, and essence of the physical body.

ATIYOGA, Skt. The last and highest of the inner tantras, the summit of the system of nine vehicles according to the Nyingma classification; a synonym of the Great Perfection (Dzogchen), which represents the ultimate view of the Nyingma school: the union of primordial purity (*ka dag*) and spontaneous presence (*lhun grub*), in other words, of voidness and awareness. Its innermost secret teachings are the Heart Essence teachings.

AVALOKITESHVARA, Skt., *spyan ras gzigs*. The "Lord Who Sees," name of the bodhisattva who embodies the speech and compassion of all the buddhas; the *sambhogakaya* emanation of the Buddha Amitabha.

BODHICHITTA, Skt., *byang chub kyi sems*. On the relative level, this is the wish to attain buddhahood for the sake of all sentient beings, together with the practice necessary to accomplish this. On the absolute level, it is nondual wisdom, the ultimate nature of the mind and the true status of all phenomena. In certain tantric contexts, bodhichitta refers to the essential physical substance that is the support of the mind.

BODHISATTVA, Skt., *byang chub sems dpa'*. One who through compassion strives to attain the full enlightenment of buddhahood for the sake of all beings. Bodhisattvas may be "ordinary" or "noble," depending on whether or not they have attained the path of seeing and are residing on one of the ten bodhisattva grounds.

BUDDHA, Skt., *sangs rgyas*. The Fully Awakened One, a being who has removed the emotional and cognitive veils, and is endowed with all enlightened qualities of realization.

BUDDHAFIELD, *zhing khams*. From a certain point of view a buddhafield is a sphere or dimension manifested by buddhas or great bodhisattvas, in which beings may abide and progress towards enlightenment without ever falling into lower states of existence. However, anywhere viewed as the pure manifestation of spontaneous wisdom is a buddhafield.

CHAKRAVARTIN, Skt., *'khor lo sgyur ba'i rgyal po*. A universal king or "wheel-monarch," the name given to a special kind of exalted being who has dominion over a greater or smaller part of the three thousand-fold universe, so called because he is said to possess a great wheel-shaped weapon with which he subdues his enemies. According to traditional cosmology, such beings appear only when the human life span surpasses eighty thousand years. By analogy, the word is also used as a title for a great king.

CREATION AND PERFECTION STAGES. The two principal phases of tantric practice. The creation stage (*bskyed rim*) involves meditation on appearances, sounds, and thoughts as deities, mantras, and wisdom, respectively. The perfection stage (*rdzogs rim*) refers to the dissolution of visualized forms into emptiness and the experience of this. It also indicates the meditation on the subtle channels, energies, and essential substances of the body.

DHARMA, Skt., *chos*. This Sanskrit term is most commonly used to indicate the doctrine of the Buddha. The term actually has ten meanings. The Dharma of transmission refers to the corpus of verbal teachings, whether oral or written. The Dharma of realization refers to the spiritual qualities resulting from practicing these teachings.

DIAMOND VEHICLE, *rdo rje theg pa*. *See* Vajrayana.

DHARMAKAYA, Skt., *chos sku*. *See* Kaya.

DOWNFALL, *ltung ba*. A transgression of one of the precepts, which if not properly confessed and repaired will result in rebirth in the lower realms.

EMPOWERMENT, *dbang*; *abhisheka*, Skt. Empowerment or initiation. Of these two terms, *initiation*, though in many ways unsatisfactory, has the advantage of indicating that it is the point of entry into tantric practice. On the other hand, *empowerment* is closer to the Tibetan word, which refers to the transference of wisdom power from the master to disciples, authorizing and enabling them to engage in the practice and reap its fruit.

EMPTINESS, *stong pa nyid*; *shunyata*, Skt. This central notion of Mahayana Buddhism refers to the ultimate nature of phenomena beyond the four ontological extremes.

GREAT PERFECTION, *rdzogs pa chen po*; *mahasandhi*, Skt. *See* Atiyoga.

GREAT VEHICLE, *theg pa chen po*. *See* Mahayana.

GURU RINPOCHE. *See* Padmasambhava.

GURU YOGA, Skt., *bla ma'i rnal 'byor*. A practice consisting of the visualization of the guru (in whichever form), prayers and requests for blessing, the visualized reception of these blessings, and the merging of the mind in the guru's enlightened wisdom mind. Guru yoga is the single most important practice of tantric Buddhism.

HEART ESSENCE, *snying thig*. These are the most profound teachings of the Nyingmapa school, belonging to the innermost cycle of the secret section of the pith instruction class of the atiyoga. They were brought to Tibet by Guru Padmasambhava and Vimalamitra.

HINAYANA, *theg dman*. The fundamental system of Buddhist thought and practice deriving from the first turning of the wheel of Dharma and centering around the teachings on the four noble truths and the twelvefold chain of dependent arising. It should be noted that in Tibetan Buddhism, the Hinayana is regarded as an intrinsic part, indeed the foundation, of the teachings and is not disparaged, even though the characteristically Hinayana motivation of aiming solely for one's own liberation (as contrasted with the universal attitude of bodhichitta), is considered incomplete and insufficient. Altogether there were eighteen Hinayana schools, of which only one, the Theravada, still exists today, mainly in the countries of South Asia.

IGNORANCE, *ma rig pa*; *avidya*, Skt. In a Buddhist context, ignorance is not mere nescience but mistaken apprehension. It is the incorrect understanding of, or failure to recognize, the ultimate nature of the person and phenomena, and falsely ascribing true existence to them.

KALPA, *bskal pa*. A great kalpa is the time period corresponding to a cycle of formation, duration, destruction, and vacuity of a universe (each of these four phases comprising twenty intermediate kalpas). There is also a so-called measureless kalpa (*grangs med bskal pa*), which, despite its name, does not refer to an infinite lapse of time, but to a specific period defined in the Abhidharma as consisting of 10^{59} kalpas. The present (great) kalpa is usually referred to as the Good or Fortunate kalpa on account of the fact that a thousand universal buddhas will appear in the course of it. The Buddha Shakyamuni is the fourth in the series.

KARMA, Skt., *las*. Action, the psychophysical principle of cause and effect according to which all experiences are the result of previous actions, and all actions are the seeds of future existential situations. Actions resulting in the experience of happiness are defined as virtuous; actions that give rise to suffering are described as nonvirtuous.

KAYA, Skt., *sku*. According to the teachings of the Mahayana, the transcendent reality of perfect buddhahood is described in terms of two or three bodies, or kayas. The two bodies, in the first case, are the dharmakaya, the body of ultimate reality, and the rupakaya, the body of form. The dharmakaya is the absolute, "emptiness" aspect of buddhahood and is perceptible only to beings on that level. The rupakaya is subdivided (thus giving rise to the three bodies mentioned above) into the sambhogakaya, the body of perfect enjoyment, and the *nirmanakaya*, the body of manifestation. The sambhogakaya, or the spontaneous clarity aspect of buddhahood, is perceptible only to highly realized beings. The nirmanakaya, the compassionate aspect, is perceptible to ordinary beings and appears in the world in human form, although not exclusively.

LAMA, *bla ma*. Tibetan term for a highly realized spiritual teacher, the equivalent of the Sanskrit word *guru*. In the colloquial language, however, it is sometimes used as a polite way of addressing a monk.

LANGDARMA. Brother of the religious king Tri Ralpachen. When the latter was murdered by his Bönpo ministers in the year 906, Langdarma became king. He persecuted Buddhism and almost succeeded in eradicating it, especially in its monastic form. After six years of rule he was assassinated by a Buddhist yogi.

LOWER REALMS, *ngan song*. The hell realms, and those of famished spirits and animals.

MAHAYANA, Skt., *theg pa chen po*. The Great Vehicle, the tradition of Buddhism practiced mostly in the countries of northern Asia, China, Japan, Korea, Mongolia, Tibet, and the Himalayan regions. The characteristic of Mahayana is the profound view of the emptiness of all phenomena, coupled with universal compassion and the desire to deliver all beings from suffering and its causes. To this purpose, the goal of the Mahayana is the attainment of the supreme enlightenment of buddhahood, and the path consists of the practice of the six *paramitas*. On the philosophical level, the Mahayana comprises two principal schools, Madhyamika and Chittamatra, or Yogachara. The Vajrayana is a branch of the Mahayana.

MAHAYOGA, Skt. The first of the three inner tantras according to the Nyingma classification. Its chief tantra is the *Guhyagarbha*, which expounds the view of purity and equality (*dag mnyam chen po*), a central principle of the Vajrayana. All appearances in their purity are the mandala of the kayas and wisdoms. This comprises the superior relative truth. Being pure, they are all equal, wisdom and emptiness united. This is superior absolute truth. The "pure" status of the appearing mode and the "equal" status of the absolute mode of being are present indivisibly in every phenomenon. This is referred to as the great dharmakaya.

MANDALA, Skt., *dkyil 'khor*. This word has several levels of meaning. At its most basic level, it may be understood simply as a configuration or intelligible unit of space. The mandala of the deity is the sacred area or palace of the wisdom deity. The mandala of a lama might be considered as his place of residence and the retinue of disciples that surround him. The offering mandala is the entire arrangement of an offering, either in real terms or in the imagination, as when a practitioner offers the entire universe.

MANI. The six-syllable mantra of Avalokiteshvara, *Om mani padme hung*.

MERIT, *bsod nams*. Positive energy arising from wholesome action or virtue (*dge ba*). There are two kinds of merit: (1) mere "merit tending to happiness" (*bsod nams tsam po pa* or *bsod nams cha mthun*), and (2) "merit tending to liberation" (*thar pa cha mthun*), on the basis of which the mind progresses toward emancipation from samsara. "Stainless merit" (*zag med dge ba*) is "merit tending to liberation," accumulated on the five paths.

NIRVANA, Skt., *myang ngan 'das*. Lit. the state beyond suffering. As a blanket term, this indicates the various levels of enlightenment attainable in both the Shravakayana and Mahayana, namely the enlightenment of the shravakas, pratyekabuddhas, and buddhas. It should be noted, however, that when nirvana or enlightenment is understood simply as emancipation from samsara (the goal, in other words, of the Hinayana), it is not to be understood as buddhahood. As expounded in the Mahayana, buddhahood utterly transcends both the suffering of samsara and the peace of nirvana. Buddhahood is therefore referred to as "nonabiding nirvana" (*mi gnas myang 'das*), in other words, a state that abides neither in the extreme of samsara nor in that of quiescence.

PADMASAMBHAVA, *pad ma 'byung gnas*. Lit. lotus-born. Referred to by many other titles, such as the Master of Orgyen and Guru Rinpoche, Padmasambhava was predicted by the Buddha Shakyamuni as the one who would propagate the teachings of the Vajrayana. Invited to Tibet by King Trisong Detsen in the eighth century, he succeeded in definitively establishing there the Buddhist teachings of sutra and tantra.

PRATIMOKSHA, Skt., *so sor thar pa*. Lit. individual liberation. This term is used to refer to the eight kinds of Buddhist ordination, together with their connected vows and disciplines.

PRATYEKABUDDHA, Skt., *rang sangs rgyas*. A "solitary buddha," one who without relying on a teacher but through the power of past karma attains the cessation of suffering by meditating on the twelve links of dependent arising. A pratyekabuddha realizes the emptiness of the personal self and goes halfway to realizing the emptiness of phenomena. In other words, he realizes the emptiness of external, perceived, phenomena. The emptiness of the subject (the perceiving mind) remains to be realized.

PURE LAND, *zhing khams*. *See* Buddhafield.

PURE PERCEPTION, *dag snang*. The perception of the world as the pure display of the kayas and wisdoms, in other words, as a buddhafield. Tending in this same direction is the contrived pure perception of a practitioner who endeavors to view everything purely, while still on the conceptual level.

RABJUNG, *rab byung*. Period of time used to count eras, consisting of sixty years.

RUPAKAYA, Skt., *gzugs sku*. Form body. *See* Kaya.

SADHANA, Skt., *sgrub thabs*. Method of accomplishment. A tantric meditative practice involving visualization of deities and the recitation of mantras.

SAMANTABHADRA, *kun tu bzang po*. Primordial buddha who has

never fallen in delusion; a symbol of awareness; the ever present pure and luminous nature of the mind.

SAMAYA, Skt., *dam tsig.* The sacramental bond and commitment in the Vajrayana established between the master and the disciples on whom empowerment is conferred. The samaya bond also exists between the disciples of the same master and between disciples and their practice.

SAMSARA, Skt., *'khor ba.* The wheel or round of existence. The state of being unenlightened, in which the mind, enslaved by the three poisons of desire, anger, and ignorance, evolves uncontrolled from one state to another, passing through an endless stream of psychophysical experiences, all of which are characterized by suffering.

SANGHA, Skt., *dge 'dun.* The community of Buddhist practitioners, whether monastic or lay. The term *noble sangha* refers to those members of the Buddhist community who have attained the path of seeing and beyond.

SECRET MANTRA, *gsang sngags. See* Vajrayana.

SHAKYAMUNI. Gautama, the historical Buddha of our age, the founder of Buddhism.

SHANTARAKSHITA, *zhi ba mtsho.* Also known as Khenpo Bodhisattva. Associated with the monastic university of Nalanda, Shantarakshita was the great exponent of the Yogachara-Svatantrika-Madhyamika school. He visited Tibet in the eighth century at the invitation of King Trisong Detsen and ordained the first seven Tibetan monks. It was at the suggestion of Shantarakshita that the king invited Guru Rinpoche to Tibet.

SHRAVAKA, Skt., *nyan thos.* One who hears the teachings of the Buddha, practices them, and transmits them to others—with a view to his or her personal liberation from samsara, rather than the perfect enlightenment of buddhahood. Shravakas are practitioners of the root vehicle, Hinayana, which is often for that reason called the Shravakayana.

SUGATAGARBHA, Skt., *bde gshegs snying po*. The essence of buddhahood, the luminous and empty nature of the mind.

SUTRA, Skt., *mdo*. A Buddhist scripture, a transcribed discourse of the Buddha. There are Hinayana and Mahayana sutras (which are distinct from the tantras).

TANTRA, Skt., *rgyud*. Lit. continuum. These are the texts of Vajrayana Buddhism expounding the natural purity of the mind. The Nyingma school classifies the tantras into outer tantras (kriya, upa, and yoga) and inner tantras (mahayoga, anuyoga, and atiyoga). The Sarma tradition uses another method, dividing the tantras into four classes: kriya, upa, and yoga tantras, and anuttaratantra.

TATHAGATAGARBHA, Skt., *de bzhin gshegs pa'i snying po*. See Sugatagarbha.

THREE REALMS, *khams gsum*. A categorization of samsaric existence: (1) the world of desire, consisting of the six existential states, from the hells up to the second sphere of the god realm; (2) the divine world of form; and (3) the divine world of nonform.

TUSHITA, Skt., *dga' ldan*. The joyous realm. The fourth divine sphere of the desire realm, in which Buddha Shakyamuni abode before appearing in our world.

VAJRA KINDRED, *rdo rje spun*. Spiritual brothers and sisters or fellow practitioners in the Vajrayana. The closest kinship is between those who receive the empowerment in the same mandala from the same teacher.

VAJRASATTVA, Skt., *rdo rje sems dpa'*. Generally speaking, the sambhogakaya buddha of the vajra family. Meditation on Vajrasattva is a powerful method for the purification of defilements. In the

Nyingma tradition, moreover, Vajrasattva is considered to be the sovereign of all yidam deities; his mantra "contains" the mantras of all deities.

VAJRAYANA, Skt., *rdo rje theg pa*. A corpus of teachings and practices based on the tantras, scriptures that discourse upon the primordial purity of the mind.

VEHICLE, *theg pa, yana*, Skt. A system of teachings providing means for traveling the path to enlightenment. There are three main vehicles: Shravakayana, Pratyekabuddhayana, and Bodhisattvayana. The Vajrayana is included in the Bodhisattvayana.

VIMALAMITRA, *dri med bshes gnyen*. One of the greatest masters and scholars of Indian Buddhism in general and of the Heart Essence in particular. He went to Tibet in the ninth century, where he taught and translated numerous Sanskrit texts.

VINAYA, Skt., *'dul ba*. The name of the Buddhist ethical teachings in general, and in particular the code of monastic discipline.

WISDOMS, *ye shes lnga*. The five wisdoms of buddhahood corresponding to the five Dhyani buddhas or five buddha families: the mirrorlike wisdom (Vajrasattva, vajra family), wisdom of equality (Ratnasambhava, the jewel family), all-discerning wisdom (Amitabha, the lotus family), all-accomplishing wisdom (Amogasiddhi, the action family), and wisdom of *dharmadhatu* (Vairochana, the tathagata family).

YIDAM, *yi dam*. A meditational deity, in male or female form, representing different aspects of enlightenment. Yidams may be peaceful or wrathful, and are meditated upon according to the nature and needs of the individual practitioner.

N OTES

1. *Kyabje* (*skyabs rje*), which means "lord of refuge," is the traditional title given to lamas of great wisdom and attainment. Curiously enough, in situations where it is traditionally used, there has been a tendency in western Europe and America to substitute the papal title of "His Holiness." Although there is perhaps some justification for this when referring to the Dalai Lama (temporal and spiritual leadership and by now a precedent of almost a hundred years), its generalized employment, along with that of other titles taken from the Catholic hierarchy, seems for a number of reasons out of place and undesirable. It should be remembered that "His Holiness" and "His Eminence" are essentially indications of ecclesiastical rank, bestowed by authority and not by popular acclaim. Moreover, they are not automatically regarded as expressions of devotion, nor are they necessarily attestations of spiritual attainment or personal sanctity, as should be clear from even a cursory knowledge of Catholic history. It seems better, therefore, to retain the Tibetan title, which, when

used of a lama like Dudjom Rinpoche, is highly meaningful and indeed an exact description.

2. Three vehicles, *theg pa gsum*, the vehicles of shravakas, pratyekabuddhas, and bodhisattvas. According to the Hinayana and Chittamatra point of view, these three vehicles are final paths and correspond to three fixed types of beings. By contrast, the Madhyamika teaches that the three vehicles correspond to what is merely a temporary orientation and that in the last analysis there is only one vehicle leading to buddhahood. This means that after accomplishing the fruit of their path, which is not, as they believe, final, the shravakas and pratyekabuddhas are at length roused from the peace of their nirvana and enter the Mahayana. They then follow the bodhisattva path and attain buddhahood.

3. An emanation "compassionately appearing from above" (*thugs rjes yas sprul*) is a *tulku*, or manifestation of a fully enlightened being who freely enters the world in order to help beings. It is to be distinguished from the rebirth of a lama or teacher who is still progressing on the path and who has not yet attained complete buddhahood (*lam rim gyis bgrod pa'i bla ma*).

4. All supreme nirmanakaya buddhas display twelve deeds. (1) They descend from Tushita, (2) enter the womb of the mother, and (3) take birth. (4) They learn all sciences and arts and, when adults, (5) delight in the company of their consorts. (6) They renounce worldly life and (7) practice austerities. (8) They go to Vajrasana, (9) vanquish the hosts of *mara*s, and (10) achieve perfect enlightenment. (11) They then turn the wheel of Dharma and (12) at length pass into nirvana.

5. The Hinayana and general Mahayana are called causal vehicles because those who practice them work only with the

causes that directly produce the result of their path (arhat-ship in the case of the shravakas) and indirectly produce the final result of buddhahood. The resultant vehicle (Vajrayana) is so called because it is the path on which practitioners work with the result itself, namely the empty, luminous nature of the mind.

6. The lowest of the hot hells, according to Buddhist teaching, characterized by the most intense and protracted form of suffering.

7. The subtle structure of the physical body consists of a system of channels in which the wind-energies circulate, transport-ing the essence drops that are the support of the mind. To adopt an upright posture has a direct influence on the state of one's mind.

8. Here Dudjom Rinpoche is referring more to the "Dharma of realization," the spiritual qualities gained through imple-menting the "Dharma of transmission," the teachings.

9. The primordial citadel refers to the ever present pure and luminous nature of the mind, which has never fallen and will never fall into delusion—in other words, pure awareness, or rigpa.

10. Date supplied by Trulshik Rinpoche, who was present at the event.

11. The texts, mostly tantric, of the kahma collection of the Nying-ma school were compiled by Terdag Lingpa Gyurme Dorje (1646-1714), the founder of Mindroling monastery, and his brother Lochen Dharma Shri (1654-1717). The collection was first printed at Dzogchen monastery by Gyalse Zhenpen Thaye (1800-?), who established the annual seven-day prac-tice on each of the thirteen major mandalas of the kahma cycle.

12. The various schools of Tibetan Buddhism are broadly classi-
fied into two main groups referred to as Nyingma (old) and
Sarma (new). Strictly speaking, as Dudjom Rinpoche says,
this refers to the work of translating Buddhist texts from
Sanskrit into Tibetan. The Nyingma school, of which Dudjom Rinpoche was the recognized leader, goes back to the
earliest period, whereas the Sarma schools, that is, the Sakya,
Kagyu, and Gelug, were founded in later centuries following
the reestablishment of Buddhism in Tibet after a period of
persecution.

13. As narrated in *Lady of the Lotus-Born*, the religious king Trisong
Detsen (790–844) wished to establish the Buddhadharma in
Tibet, following the example of his forefather Songtsen
Gampo. He therefore invited from India the famous Mahayana scholar and abbot Shantarakshita, who began the project
of building the first Buddhist monastery in Tibet. Seeing that
his endeavors were attended by many obstacles due to
Bönpo ministers and other negative forces, he advised the
king to ask the assistance of the tantric master Guru Padmasambhava. The latter came to Tibet and brought the obstruc-
tive powers under control. He thus firmly established the
Dharma in Tibet and instructed his disciples, including the
king, in the tantric and Dzogchen teachings. In order to test
whether the Tibetans were capable of upholding the vows,
seven men (the so-called seven men who were tried) were
selected and ordained by Shantarakshita, and the work of
translating the Sanskrit scriptures began on a grand scale.
Many Indian masters and authorities were invited to Tibet,
to teach and help in this work. One of the greatest of these
was the scholar and Dzogchen master Vimalamitra, who
taught, and himself translated, many tantric and Dzogchen

texts, among them the *Mayajala-tantra* of the mahayoga and the texts of the Heart Essence of the atiyoga. The Tibetans also contributed mightily to the work. Many studied Sanskrit and became translators. Of these, Vairotsana was preeminent. He was a monk—one of the first seven—and studied in India with the Dzogchen master Shri Singha. He also received the teachings of the Dzogchen tantras in a pure vision from Garab Dorje himself, and among other things, translated the five earlier tantras of the mind section of atiyoga. Kawa Peltsek (another of the seven who were tried) was also a great practitioner and translator, both on his own account and also in collaboration with Vimalamitra, from whom he received the teachings of Heart Essence. Chokro Lui Gyaltsen was a close disciple of both Guru Padmasambhava and Vimalamitra, from whom he received the teachings of Heart Essence. Ma Rinchen Chok, also one of the seven who were tried, succeeded Shantarakshita as the head of the Tibetan monastic sangha. He was one of the scholars (in the group headed by Kamalashila) who defeated the Chinese master Hashang in the famous debate at Samye. Nyak Jñana Kumara, ordained by Shantarakshita, was a great scholar and translator and an accomplished master. He was the first of the three great masters (the other two were [1] Nubchen Sangye Yeshe and [2] the three masters of the Zur clan, who are counted together as one) who received all the transmissions of the mahayoga, the anuyoga, and the mind section of the atiyoga teachings. Trisong Detsen had three sons, Muni Tsenpo, Murub Tsenpo, and Mutig (or Mutri) Tsenpo, who all became great Buddhist leaders. Mutig Tsenpo's son was Tri Ralpachen, the last great religious king of the Chogyal dynasty. For more information see Dudjom Rinpoche, *The*

Nyingma School of Buddhism (Boston: Wisdom Publications, 1991); Gyalwa Changchub and Namkhai Nyingpo, *Lady of the Lotus-Born* (Boston: Shambhala Publications, 1999); Tulku Thondup, *The Tantric Tradition of the Nyingmapa* (Marion, Mass.: Buddhayana, 1984); and Tulku Thondup, *Masters of Meditation and Miracles* (Boston: Shambhala Publications, 1996).

14.   Langdarma was the elder brother of the Buddhist king Tri Ralpachen (866–901), whom he murdered. He was a Bönpo, an adherent of the aboriginal, pre-Buddhist religion of Tibet, and his rule, from 901 to 906, was marked by the wholesale destruction of Buddhist institutions, in particular the monastic order. He was in turn assassinated by the Buddhist yogi Lhalung Pelgyi Dorje. Shortly after his death, his junior queen gave birth to a son, Ösung, who was later enthroned in Lhasa. In due course, this led to a rebellion, provoked by the alleged son of the senior queen, and a further division of the dynasty was later caused by Ösung's two grandsons. This led to the fragmentation of the kingdom, and the royal lineage survived only in western Tibet, where one of Ösung's grandsons was exiled. A descendent of this lineage, Tsenpo Khoré, held power there but later abdicated in favor of his younger brother in order to become a Buddhist monk, taking the name Lha Lama Yeshe Ö. Yeshe Ö sent twenty-one young men to Kashmir to learn Sanskrit and study the Dharma. Of these, only two survived the journey and later became famous translators: Rinchen Zangpo, the first Sarma translator (958–1051) and Lekpe Sherab. Later on, Yeshe Ö sent an invitation accompanied by presents of gold to Atisha Dipamkara, a great Mahayana abbot of the monastic university of Vikramashila in India. Atisha first declined the invitation and the gifts, on the grounds that his presence was

necessary in India to prevent the further decline of the Buddhadharma. Several years later he accepted a second invitation, realizing the immense effort and trouble Yeshe Ö and his people went through in order to request his presence. Atisha remained in Tibet for twelve years and died there in 1054 at the monastery of Nyethang. From Atisha and his disciple Dromtönpa originated a new movement in Tibetan Buddhism, the Kadampa school.

15. This great tantric master (*gnub chen sangs rgyas ye shes*), who on his own account attained the age of 130, was the second of the three greatest masters who consolidated and propagated the tantric teachings in Tibet. (The first was Nyak Jñana Kumara, while the three masters of the Zur clan are counted all together as the third.) Nubchen Sangye Yeshe was a disciple of Guru Padmasambhava and Nyag Jñana Kumara and displayed many miraculous signs of accomplishment. He visited India and Nepal, and received teachings from Shri Singha, Vimalamitra, and others. It is said that when Langdarma began his work of destruction, he summoned Nubchen and asked for a demonstration of his power. In reply, the great yogi raised his hand in a wrathful mudra, and in the sky above, the king saw nine scorpions the size of yaks. The yogi then made a threatening gesture in the direction of a large rock, which was instantly shattered by lightning. The king was understandably impressed and promised not to harm him or his followers. In fact, Nubchen Sangye Yeshe had many disciples and was a prolific writer. One of his most important works was a text entitled *The Lamp of Concentration* (*bsam gtan mig sgron*), in which he demonstrates the difference between the view of Dzogchen and the teaching of Hashang, a Chinese Ch'an master who propounded the doctrine of

instantaneous enlightenment in contrast with the gradualist approach of Kamalashila, the disciple of Shantarakshita.

16. The Kadampa tradition has its origin in Atisha (982–1054) and his disciple Dromtönpa. The Sakyapa tradition was founded by Konchog Gyalpo (1034–1102), while the Kagyupas originated mainly with Marpa Lotsawa (1012–1099). Finally, Tsongkhapa (1357–1419) founded the Gelug tradition, to which the Dalai Lamas belong.

17. The first tertön to appear was Sangye Lama, in the eleventh century. He was a manifestation of King Trisong Detsen and discovered sadhanas on Guru Padmasambhava, Avalokiteshvara, and the teachings on the Great Perfection in a pillar in the Lowo Gekar temple in Ngari, west Tibet. For more information about the terma and tertöns, see Tulku Thondup, *Hidden Teachings of Tibet* (London: Wisdom Publications, 1986).

18. These are known in Tibetan as *mdo sgyu sems gsum*. *Mdo* stands for *'dus pa mdo*, the tantra of anuyoga, *sgyu* stands for the mahayoga *Mayajala-tantra (sgyu 'phrul drva ba)*, and *sems* stands principally for the mind section of atiyoga.

19. Skt. *tantra, agama* (commentary), and *upadesha* (essential instruction). In Tibetan these are *rgyud, lung, man ngag*.

20. The first collection of Nyingma tantras was made, at the cost of great effort, by Ratna Lingpa (1403–1478), followed by Terdag Lingpa (1646–1714) and his brother Lochen Dharma Shri. On the basis of their collections, Vidyadhara Jigme Lingpa (1730–1798) compiled the first catalog. In the 1970s, Dilgo Khyentse Rinpoche published *The Collection of the Nyingma Tantras (rnying ma rgyud 'bum)* in thirty-three volumes.

21. *bka' brgyad*. Among the sadhanas of the Eight Great Herukas there are three major cycles: *bka' brgyad bde gshegs 'dus pa*, dis-

covered by Nyang Nyima Özer (1124-1192); *bka' brgyad gsang ba yongs rdzogs* of Guru Chowang (1212-1270); and *bka' brgyad drag po rang byung rang shar* of Rigdzin Godem (1337-1408). These termas are all *sa gter*, or earth treasures, which means that their revelation was prompted by the discovery of material objects in the ground, and so forth—as distinct from *dgongs gter*, or mind treasures, in which the teaching manifests directly in the mind of the tertön. See Tulku Thondup's *Hidden Teachings of Tibet*.

22. *bla ma dgongs 'dus*, a famous and very large earth treasure cycle consisting of thirteen volumes, discovered by Sangye Lingpa (1340-1396).

23. This refers mainly to the so-called *spu gri* sadhana discovered by Guru Chowang and the *yangs gsang bla med* sadhana (Raling Purba) of Ratna Lingpa.

24. This is the root text of all the mahayoga tantras. Its full name is *rdo rje sems dpa' sgyu 'phrul drva ba rtsa ba'i rgyud gsang ba snying po*, the root tantra of *Vajrasattva's Phantasmagorical Net—The Secret Essence*.

25. *tshogs chen 'dus pa*.

26. *sems smad ma bu bco brgyad*, "eighteen texts like mother and children." The first five tantras, translated by Vairotsana, are like a mother, and the thirteen later tantras, translated by Yudra Nyingpo and Guru Padmasambhava, are like her children.

27. *rdo rje zam pa*.

28. *rgyud bco bdun*.

29. It was from Minling Chung Rinpoche Ngawang Chödrak that Trulshik Rinpoche, the great holder of the Nyingma eastern lineage of monastic transmission, received his vows.

30. Vajradhara (*rdo rje 'chang*), lit. holder of the vajra, is a highly

respectful way of addressing a great teacher. It is the teacher who holds the key to our indestructible (vajra) nature. Dudjom Rinpoche is referring here to Khenpo Aten, Gyurme Pende Ösel.

31. *rin chen gter gyi mdzod*, a collection of termas of all major tertöns of the Nyingma school, compiled by Kongtrul Lodro Thaye (1813–1899) in sixty volumes. Dilgo Khyentse Rinpoche added some further volumes and published the whole revised collection in Delhi in 1978.

32. Gyurme Ngedön Wangpo, the disciple of Dudjom Lingpa and one of the root teachers of Dudjom Rinpoche.

33. Jamyang Khyentse Wangpo (1820–1892) was the initiator of the *ris med* or nonsectarian movement in Tibet. A great scholar in all the Tibetan traditions and an accomplished master, he was one of the few major tertöns who held all seven streams of transmission (*bka' 'babs chu bo bdun*), namely the teachings of the kahma transmission and the six kinds of terma transmission. For this reason, he is known as the last of the five great tertön kings.

34. Kongtrul Lodro Thaye (1813–1899), an outstanding scholar, master, and tertön, is closely associated with Jamyang Khyentse Wangpo in the nonsectarian movement. He was a prolific writer who compiled teachings on a large variety of subjects. Another of his major works is known as the *Five Great Treasuries (mdzod chen lnga)*.

35. It is recorded that, amazingly, Dudjom Rinpoche was fourteen years old when he gave the *rin chen gter mdzod* for the first time.

36. *dag pa rab 'byams*, a technical term referring to the tantric realization that appearances, sounds, and thoughts are the mandala of the deities, mantras, and primordial wisdom.

37. The fourteen root downfalls of the common unsurpassable tantras (as listed by Ashvaghosha) are:

    1. to criticize and disparage masters from whom one received the teachings of the Vajrayana;
    2. to transgress the precepts given by the Buddha, regarding things to implement and reject, and to ignore the words of an authentic teacher;
    3. to be angry with one's vajra kindred;
    4. to harm beings or to forsake love for beings;
    5. to lose bodhichitta in all its forms;
    6. to deride other Buddhist traditions and non-Buddhist religions;
    7. to divulge the secret teachings to improper recipients;
    8. to have contempt for one's body and the other skandhas;
    9. to doubt the teachings about the pure nature of all phenomena;
    10. to refrain from "liberating" harmful beings and negative forces;
    11. to conceptualize that which is beyond any designation;
    12. to scandalize the faithful, thus making them turn away from the teachings;
    13. to neglect the proper use of samaya substances;
    14. to deride women.

38. The three roots, *rtsa gsum*, are the three objects of refuge as expressed in the tantric teachings. These are the guru, who is the root of blessings; the yidam, the root of accomplishment; and the dakini, the root of activities.

39. A talk given by Dudjom Rinpoche to his monastic and lay disciples on the occasion of the empowerment of the *Distillation of the Seven Treasure Teachings, bla sgrub gter kha bdun bsdus*,

which is a sadhana composed by Dudjom Rinpoche on the basis of seven terma practices centered on Guru Padmasambhava.

40. During the reign of Songtsen Gampo (617–698), the Tibetan script and the first Tibetan grammar were devised by Thonmi Sambhota, and the first Buddhist scriptures, relating to Avalokiteshvara and so on, were translated. This laid the ground for Buddhist practice and meditation. Songtsen Gampo also built two of Tibet's most important temples, the Jo-Khang and Ramoche, to house the images of Buddha Shakyamuni and the Buddha Akshobya, brought to Tibet by Songtsen Gampo's wives, Gyasa, a princess from China, and Belsa, a princess from Nepal.

41. *sa*, ground or level, and *lam*, path. The practice of the Mahayana is divided into five paths (of accumulation, joining, seeing, meditation, and no-more-learning), which are gradually traversed as the practitioner progresses toward buddhahood. The third path, that of seeing, is the point where the practitioner has a direct experience of ultimate reality. There then begins a second system of grounds or levels of bodhisattva realization, which extends from the path of seeing through the path of meditation and culminates in the attainment of the path of no-more-learning, buddhahood.

42. A *tsatsa* is a small stupa, statue of Buddha, and the like, made by pressing clay into a mold.

43. Pretas, *yi dvags*, are famished spirits, one of the six classes of beings in samsara.

44. That is, representations of the Three Jewels, the Lama, sacred images, books, and so forth.

45. The fifth Dalai Lama (1617–1682), Gyalwa Ngawang Lozang Gyatso, often referred to as the Great Fifth, was the first

Dalai Lama to become the ruler of the whole of Tibet. He had strong spiritual links with Terdag Lingpa and was himself a tertön. Although he was one of the principle hierarchs of the Gelugpa, he was a great protector of the Nyingmapas.

46. The thirteenth Dalai Lama (1876-1933), Gyalwa Tubten Gyatso, is known to the Tibetans as the Great Thirteenth. As well as being a great spiritual leader and writer, he was also an astute and far-sighted politician who managed to keep Tibet independent in difficult times. He tried to modernize his country and reform the government. If his advice and policy had been heeded, the fate of Tibet would have been very different.

47. This story is narrated at length in Changchub and Nyingpo's *Lady of the Lotus-Born*.

48. Tibetans, as a rule, do not use the term Dalai Lama, preferring a variety of other respectful titles. Gyalwa Rinpoche, the Precious Conqueror, is the most common.

49. *las kyi rlung*, the impure energy generated by previous actions performed in the state of ignorance, which propels one into further existence.

50. It is important to transfer the consciousness at the right time, specifically, after the respiration has stopped and before the reabsorption of the inner pulse. If the transference of consciousness is done too early, the dying person can be greatly disturbed and harmed.

51. *'byung ba lnga*, earth, air, fire, water, and space, the principles of solidity, motility, heat, liquidity, and so forth.

52. *'od gsal ma bu 'phrad*, the "mother luminosity" is the ever present fundamental expanse of absolute, empty luminosity, the nature of the mind, the primordially pure dharmakaya. Practitioners who are introduced to this absolute luminosity by

an authentic teacher and who meditate on it are able to experience luminosity as the result of their practice. This is called "child luminosity." It is thanks to this that they can recognize the "mother" or ultimate luminosity when this manifests at the moment of death. This recognition is described metaphorically as "a child climbing into its mother's lap." The mother luminosity appears to all dying sentient beings. But if they have not meditated on it and are therefore unfamiliar with it, they experience only a brief flash. It is instantly lost, unrecognized in the sequences of hallucinatory perceptions that immediately follow.

53.   The experience of blackness arises after the white and red essences mingle in the heart center and the consciousness dissolves into them.

54.   These are not to be understood as gods in the ordinary sense of the word. Appearing in infinite peaceful and wrathful forms, they represent different aspects of the buddha-nature.

55.   It is said that the consciousness leaves the body at a point symbolically corresponding to the samsaric realm in which it will be reborn.

56.   *rdo rje gdan*, lit. indestructible vajra seat. This normally refers to Bodhgaya in India, where all the buddhas of this Fortunate kalpa (Shakyamuni included) attain enlightenment beneath the Bodhi tree. However, since the actual "place" of enlightenment is within the nature of the mind, the present remark is interpreted as meaning that empty awareness is inaccessible to the bardo consciousness, which is by definition errant and deluded.

57.   Sukhavati is the pure land of Amitabha, Abhirati is the pure land of Vajrasattva, and the Glorious Copper-Colored Mountain is the pure land of Guru Padmasambhava.

58. This refers to the practices known as *shyang chog*, purification rituals, or more particularly *gnas lung*, leading the bardo consciousness to the higher states.

59. Dudjom Lingpa (also referred to as Dudul Dorje, 1835-1903) was the manifestation of Khyeuchung Lotsawa, one of the twenty-five disciples of Padmasambhava. An accomplished yogi and teacher, he discovered many termas and had many disciples who attained the rainbow body.

60. There are five enlightened families, namely: Tathagata, Vajra, Jewel, Lotus, and Action. They are presided over by five Dhyani buddhas (respectively Vairochana, Vajrasattva, Ratnasambhava, Amitabha, and Amogasiddhi) and represent five aspects of buddhahood.

61. The three impurities of generosity can be said to refer to the preparation, the actual action of giving, and the conclusion of the act. It means that (1) the gift derives from wrong livelihood; (2) the act of giving is done with a wrong intention; (3) the donor is not happy with his act and experiences regret.

62. *mtho ris yon tan bdun*, longevity, perfect health, beauty, fortune, good family or social status, wealth, and intelligence are the qualities of the higher realms.

63. *phags pa'i nor bdun*. These have all just been mentioned in the text: faith, ethical discipline, generosity, learning, sense of shame, sense of propriety with regard to others, and clear intelligence or wisdom.

64. *chos dred*. The Tibetan expression indicates a person who knows the Dharma (perhaps very well) but has not assimilated it, and who becomes casual and unreceptive to the teacher and the teachings.

65. *'du shes* or *shes bya gsum*. "The three specific perceptions" is a reference to the practice associated with the third initiation.

66. Pemakö is situated in the south of Tibet, not far from the border with Assam. It is generally referred to as a hidden land (*sbas yul*), that is, a place or zone blessed and sealed by Guru Padmasambhava, and thus protected from violation and even entry by beings who lack the proper karmic connection. However, the region is divided into two areas: "outer Pemakö" and "inner Pemakö." The former is inhabited by ordinary beings, and though difficult to reach, may be entered. Inner Pemakö, however, remains a hidden land and only persons who are exceptionally qualified are able to gain access to it. Dudjom Rinpoche was born in "outer Pemakö."

67. In other words, the kahma and terma teachings.

Printed in the United States
by Baker & Taylor Publisher Services